BEFORE
YOU
SAY YES...

BEFORE YOU SAY YES...

A Guide to the Pleasures and Pitfalls of Volunteer Boards

DOREEN PENDGRACS

FOREWORD BY MARIAN HEBB

DUNDURN PRESS
TORONTO

Editor: Allison Hirst
Designer: Jennifer Scott
Printer: Transcontinental

Library and Archives Canada Cataloguing in Publication

Pendgracs, Doreen
    Before you say yes-- : a guide to the pleasures and pitfalls of volunteer boards / by Doreen Pendgracs.

ISBN 978-1-55488-703-3

1. Associations, institutions, etc.--Management. 2. Boards of directors. 3. Voluntarism. I. Title.

HN49.V64P45 2010   658'.048   C2009-907454-0

1   2   3   4   5   14   13   12   11   10

 Conseil des Arts du Canada   Canada Council for the Arts   Canadä   ONTARIO ARTS COUNCIL CONSEIL DES ARTS DE L'ONTARIO

We acknowledge the support of the **Canada Council for the Arts** and the **Ontario Arts Council** for our publishing program. We also acknowledge the financial support of the **Government of Canada** through the **Book Publishing Industry Development Program** and **The Association for the Export of Canadian Books**, and the **Government of Ontario** through the **Ontario Book Publishers Tax Credit program**, and the **Ontario Media Development Corporation**.

Care has been taken to trace the ownership of copyright material used in this book. The author and the publisher welcome any information enabling them to rectify any references or credits in subsequent editions.

J. Kirk Howard, President

Printed and bound in Canada.
www.dundurn.com

Dundurn Press
3 Church Street, Suite 500
Toronto, Ontario, Canada
M5E 1M2

Gazelle Book Services Limited
White Cross Mills
High Town, Lancaster, England
LA1 4XS

Dundurn Press
2250 Military Road
Tonawanda, NY
U.S.A. 14150

CONTENTS

FOREWORD

If you are reading this, you have probably already said "yes" to an invitation to become a director, or are seriously thinking of doing so, and now you have in your hands a practical introduction to the world of non-profit boards. You already are, or are about to become, one of the thousands of persons who serve every year on volunteer boards of directors of non-profit organizations — big and small — that contribute to their communities in a myriad of ways. Whether it is big or small, good "corporate governance" increases the likelihood that an organization will be successful in carrying out the purposes for which it was established. An organization without a dedicated board of governors that functions well does not have good governance and is unlikely to achieve its goals.

Doreen Pendgracs encourages her readers to join the many volunteers who put in thousands of hours of work as directors, and to participate knowledgeably, with passion, and with a good understanding of directors' roles and responsibilities. With enthusiasm and good humour, she recounts experiences of her own and of others whose paths she has crossed — sometimes frustrating, sometimes satisfying — and conveys the joys of collaborating with others on shared goals. Doreen's book will open your eyes as a director and assist you to understand the responsibilities you are assuming, including setting goals, developing policy, reading financial statements, and managing risks. It will also help you to anticipate and avoid tribulations and troubles such as conflicts of interest and to find a position that allows you to enjoy what you are doing.

I have worked with non-profit organizations for many years, usually as a legal adviser, but sometimes as a board member myself, so I know first-hand about the hard work and "the pleasures and pitfalls" that fall to the lot of directors — what they help the organization to achieve, how much they give of themselves, and what they may get out of serving on a board of directors on a personal level. My own experience has overlapped with Doreen's, so I can attest that she always practises what she preaches (nicely) and that her book will give you guidance and confidence in carrying out your duties as a director.

Marian Hebb
Toronto
November 2009

ACKNOWLEDGEMENTS

This book has been a pleasure to write, but I never would have been able to do it without the insight provided by those who I have quoted in the various chapters and others who have volunteered their thoughts on this exciting topic. I believe their comments have added the personal depth necessary to bring each point discussed to life and increased the helpfulness to you, the reader.

My deepest thanks to the following individuals and organizations for their generous help and support on this project. They are listed in the order in which their names appear in the book: Marian Hebb, Gregg Hanson, Nathalie Kleinschmit and Global'Ease, Michael OReilly, Bonnie Zink, Maureen Cavan, Industry Canada, Bruce Wilson, John (Jay) H. Remer Jr., Roger Woloshyn, Peter Harper, Lynn Lindsay and Mark Reszel of Encon Group Inc., Otto Siebenmann, Tanya Gulliver, George Butters, Surendra Bungaroo, "Joy Halloden," Holly Henderson of Altruvest Charitable Services, Marlene Hubert and the Manitoba Government and General Employees' Union, Roy Yerex, and M. Hope Spencer.

And deepest thanks to my husband, Reg Pendgracs, who had to spend much of the summer of 2009 without me as I sat at my computer — working on this book. Thank you, Reg, for your love, support, and encouragement.

I would also like to thank the following organizations for which I have served as a director (or on a committee of the board) over the past twenty-five plus years and each organization's past and current members — from whom I have learned much: Manitoba Association of Insurance Professionals, Canadian Association of Insurance Women, Manitoba Public Insurance, Manitoba Government and General Employees' Union, Women Business Owners of Manitoba, Professional Writers Association of Canada, Access Copyright, Prairie Voices Toastmasters, Lord Selkirk Toastmasters, Toastmasters International–District 64, and the Matlock Recreation Club.

Thanks to the late, great Winston Churchill for this very appropriate and inspiring quote on volunteerism: "We make a living by what we get; we make a life by what we give."

And finally, thanks to Kirk Howard and the staff at Dundurn Press for publishing this book. The partnership formed when Canadian publishers and Canadian booksellers support Canadian creators is so important in helping keep Canadian culture strong.

AUTHOR'S NOTE

This book is not in any way meant to serve as legal advice. Nor is it intended to implicate or suggest that any one individual has inadequately filled his or her role as a director or employee of any organization mentioned or not specifically mentioned in this book.

The book is intended to be a helpful reference for any individual who is considering becoming (or already is) a director on any non-profit board in North America. It is also intended to help non-profit associations improve their practices and policies with regard to board governance.

This book is solely based on the personal experience and opinions of the author and the individuals and companies she has interviewed and quoted in this book.

The purpose of this book is to educate and entertain. No ethical judgment has been made or implied toward any individual or organization.

If you (or your organization) find yourself a party in any legal action concerning board activities or improprieties, please seek legal advice.

INTRODUCTION

This book is essentially a "Do's and Don'ts" of being on a board of directors in the non-profit and not-for-profit sector. It is intended to be a valuable resource to anyone who presently sits on a non-profit board, who may be considering taking on a board position (running for election), or who has been asked to fill a vacant board position.

It is not intended to help you establish a new board. For that, you need to consult a lawyer and establish the new board in accordance with the laws of incorporation in the jurisdiction in which you live or under which the new board will operate. Industry Canada can also help you with resources. For a terrific free online publication intended to help non-profit organizations and associations operate more effectively and efficiently, visit *www. ic.gc.ca/eic/site/cilp–pdci.nsf/eng/cl00689.html* (accessed December 2, 2009).

I have written *Before You Say Yes ...* because, having spent more than twenty-five years sitting on boards of various natures in varying capacities (from a community hall, to trade unions, "women in business" associations, and boards specific to the writing and publishing arena), I believe I have the insight necessary to demystify board obligations and governance in a clear, succinct style without any legalese to confuse the prospective or new director.

This book will teach you how to deal with difficult board members and staff, and what to find out before you say yes and accept the challenge of a new board position or renew a term on a board on which you currently serve. It will help you identify red lights within the organizational structure, within yourself, and even within the fellow directors on the board you may be joining. It will help you identify your own strengths and learn to respect the strengths of your fellow directors.

I am a firm believer in volunteerism and stepping forward to get the job done. Without volunteerism, society would be at a standstill.

Just be sure you have the answers to the important questions posed in this book, and then, if you are satisfied that the decision is right for you, say Yes! — with enthusiasm, commitment, and contentment.

1   Leave Your Hat at the Door

It's flattering to be asked, and it can be loads of fun, and certainly very rewarding in a variety of ways, but before you say yes to joining a board of directors, there are many things you must consider, and much you should know.

Is this board right for you? Will volunteering on this board challenge you and enable you to grow? Will it indulge your passions? Will it be easy for you to keep your personal loyalties in check? Is there any possible conflict of interest for you to consider? These are all questions we will discuss in this chapter.

Only You Can Decide

Knowing *when* to say yes to an invitation to join a board is crucial. You need to make sure that you are joining the board that is right for you. There are many types of non-profit boards and they will appeal to different individuals with specific talents, interests, and needs.

Does your interest lie in education? Or perhaps sports, the arts, healthcare, social services, or Native issues? There are boards in all of these sectors that will incorporate these preferences.

"It's really important to find a board that best feeds your passion," says Gregg Hanson, a philanthropist and former CEO of Wawanesa Mutual Insurance Company who spends a good chunk of his time serving on various boards in both the corporate and nonprofit sectors. Hanson currently serves on three major corporate boards in Manitoba, and is also chair of the United Way's 2010 fundraising campaign and former chair of the Winnipeg Foundation. He offers some valuable advice to prospective directors. "What really excites you?" asks Hanson. "If you do what your passion is, and spend just one hour a week volunteering in that field, collectively, we could really change the world." Hanson goes on to say that if you're not passionate about an issue, don't bother agreeing to serve a board that predominantly deals with it. It will be a waste of your time, create unnecessary frustrations for you, and not be much fun.

The experiences of seasoned board members have proven that the people who become the most fulfilled by board activities are those who have passion for the work they are involved in, and can ignite that passion in others. This enthusiasm becomes infectious and ultimately is a tremendous benefit to any organization. Choosing the right board is a very personal decision. Don't let the interests or concerns of others influence you.

"Even though my daughter is an Olympian, I am not passionate about sports. So any board with a focus on sports would not work for me," says Hanson. "And even though I love animals, I am much more concerned about social services for people. So sitting on the board of the Humane Society (SPCA) would be far better suited to someone else who is more passionate about animals."

It's important to choose a board that is compatible with your interests. It is also important to choose one that is in line with your abilities.

Nathalie Kleinschmit, a director with Global'Ease training and consulting services for non-governmental organizations, has worked with many boards: "It's best not to ask people to do something as a volunteer that resembles their job because then it's too much like work," she says. "But yet, you must capitalize on their strengths and not assign them a task that is foreign to their nature. You want to help them grow."

This is sound advice. It's quite a balancing act to ensure that the volunteer task you are choosing or being asked to accept is challenging, but not beyond the reach of your abilities. Thankfully there are a myriad of boards for us to choose from. The key is to find the right home for your passion, skills, and enthusiasm. With the right fit, there's no limit to what you can accomplish.

All for One and One for All

It's a catchy phrase, and it really applies here. When you agree to sit on a board, you are acting as a representative of that organization, collective, or association. This means that the interests, needs, and goals of that umbrella organization must come before your own as well as those of the smaller organization or association that may have sponsored your candidacy as a director on a larger board.

It's important to understand the transformation of a passionate individual, with unique needs and perhaps a limited scope of vision, to one who is an unbiased, ethical, and visionary director. This metamorphosis is an important and necessary component of the successful operations of any board.

I spent six years, from 2003 to 2009, serving as a director with Access Copyright, The Canadian Copyright Licensing Agency, established in 1988 as a collective of publishers and creators of intellectual property and visual arts. That was an interesting board to work on due to the fact that the board had eighteen members, each of whom had his or her own background and bias to contend with. This rather unique and complex board was comprised of representatives of large publishers, small publishers, trade-book publishers, educational publishers of textbooks and learned journals, as well as freelance writers, book authors, poets, playwrights, photographers, visual artists, and many others from across Canada.

Each of these members associations had the right and opportunity to put forward one (or more) of their members' names for election. Each had their own distinct perspective and a voice of equal value at the table. But you can imagine that the needs and opinions of a large multi-national publisher would be significantly different — and in many instances, diabolically opposed — from that of an independent freelance writer or photographer. That's where the biggest challenge comes in: respecting — and when necessary or appropriate, accepting — different points of view from around the table.

Although you may disagree with the opinions of another director, or dislike the way they do business or represent themselves in their industry (or community) in which they are operating, you must put personal or ideological differences aside and remember that your role as an unbiased and ethical director comes before all else when you are sitting at the board table.

You must also keep in mind that each member of the board had been nominated by his or her member association and was then formally elected by the members of the collective as a whole to sit on the board. It is at that point that each elected director must check his or her unique hat at the door, and once inside, don — with unfaltering commitment — the hat of the collective they are now representing publicly and within the organization.

That is not always an easy task. We are all human, and on occasion it becomes difficult (if not impossible) for each of us to remember that, first and foremost, we are functioning as directors of the board of the mother organization and not as biased special-interest individuals (be it writers, publishers, painters, or whatever walk of life the director may be coming from).

Which brings to mind another delicate point: declaring a conflict of interest. When you sit on a board, from time to time an issue may come to the table about which you have privileged knowledge due to family or business ties or from being an "insider" to the issue for any reason.

If your vote on an issue that is before the board will financially benefit you, your family, or your business, you must excuse yourself from the room during any discussion on the matter and be excluded from the vote. You may be consulted for background information on the issue, but you should not be a party to the decision-making discussion surrounding a motion of the board. If a potential conflict of interest situation presents itself, you must declare it openly and immediately. Even if you are unsure as to whether the situation does indeed represent an actual conflict of interest, you are better to fully disclose it before a difficult or delicate scenario results. Ask that your absence from the discussion and abstention from the vote be included in the minutes of the meeting to ensure that no unfounded allegations can be made against you, the board, or the organization.

On board matters, it is always important to be *proactive* as opposed to being *reactive*. That means speaking up before you're boxed into a corner and before any accusatory fingers get pointed in your direction.

Does Size Matter?

Board size can be a delicate subject. Although some may shriek at or question the necessity of a board with as many as eighteen members, in my experience, size does matter, and a larger board is often to the benefit of the membership.

An organization I formerly served had been carefully considering shrinking the size of its board over time, and even outside consultants had recommended that we should do so on more than one occasion. But whenever a vote was taken, the will of the majority of the board, and ultimately the members of the organization, was clearly to maintain the status quo.

Had we reduced the number of directors on the board, whose voice(s) would have been lost? Whose interests would be ignored because their segment of the industry no longer played an active role in the decision-making process?

I hear you. You're saying, "But I thought you said that directors were not supposed to vote based on their individual beliefs or the beliefs of their organization." That is true; however, you will find that often decisions for the good of the whole are made from hearing different perspectives (sometimes repeatedly), considering a variety of alternatives, and reaching consensus on what is best for the organization in its entirety. That can only happen with effort, over time, and if a diverse representation of voices is present at the policy-making table.

In my opinion, shrinking a board reduces the number of perspectives shared around the table, and in the end, if a larger board is working effectively, why "fix what ain't broke?" In search of a second opinion on this important topic, I spoke to Michael OReilly, past president of the Professional Writers Association of Canada (PWAC), co-chair of the Access Copyright board, and newly elected national president of the Canadian Freelance Union (CFU).

OReilly has sat on many student and commu-nity boards and seen how they work from the inside. Alternatively, he has worked as a journalist covering political affairs and has seen boards function — and malfunction — from an observer's point of view. "I think the challenge with board size is the rightsizing of the board. A size that may be good for one organization may not be suited to another," he says. "It depends on the scope of the tasks that the board is faced with. Some boards face such diverse issues that having diverse voices and backgrounds around the table becomes essential."

He admits that logistics and the organizing of tasks may be more challenging with a larger board, but the positive side of that argument is that larger boards often produce better and faster results, as there are a greater number of hands available to get things done more expeditiously. "There is no simple answer," he says. "You need to find the balance that helps you achieve things. And it is important to remember that the driving force is not the number of people on a board. The driving force is the needs of the organization."

OReilly also points out that regional representation is essential for certain types of organizations, particularly grassroots associations where diverse challenges from region to region strongly affect the opinions of directors originating from the various geographical regions: "Having regional representation on a board can certainly increase buy-in from the membership. It may not be necessary or suitable for all boards, but it is certainly my experience that it can be invaluable to some."

I wholeheartedly agree with that. Those of us coming from outside of central Canada have often felt excluded from the decision-making process of some larger organizations. We have, on occasion, been made to feel like disadvantaged second cousins or unwanted children in a large family.

Regional representation helps counteract that feeling, because our votes count just as much as those of someone from "the centre of the universe." Boards that allow for and encourage regional representation can therefore be considered to be more democratic. As OReilly mentioned, they may not be entirely appropriate for *all* organizations, but they are well-suited to most.

The resounding theme to remember is that no one size or board formula will fit every organization. "The goals of the board or organization will determine what criteria should be in place for board member participation and these guidelines should be well publicized so that all qualified people will feel free to apply or show their interest," says OReilly.

Tips for Board Members

- ✓ Be impartial.
- ✓ Be attentive.
- ✓ Be well-informed.
- ✓ Be innovative.
- ✓ Be fair.
- ✓ Be consultative.
- ✓ Be courteous.
- ✓ Be flexible.
- ✓ Be loyal to the organization.
- ✓ Be trustworthy.
- ✓ Be a good listener.
- ✓ Be there. Attend in-person and online meetings whenever possible.

The accountants among us may counter the argument to maintain or establish a large board by saying, "It's going to cost the organization too much to maintain this board." It is true that the costs associated with having a large board will increase the board's operating costs. But it is worth the additional cost both to the organization and to its members only if each member of the board is participating to the best of his or her abilities. Each board member must contribute by attending meetings, by accepting challenges and responsibilities, by expressing his or her opinions when the need or opportunity arises, and by acting in good faith.

And remember: it is never wrong for a board member to have an opinion or rationale that reflects his or her unique background. That should be welcomed around the board table. But every board member must ensure that he or she attentively listens to the sentiments expressed by all fellow board members. And if an opposing view makes sense once you have heard the rationale behind it, feel free to change your opinion — and your vote. This has happened to me many times over the course of my twenty-five years serving on various boards. I have entered the boardroom with a specific take on an issue that will be discussed, but after hearing the arguments of my fellow board members, I have felt confident that their position on the issue was more logical, relevant, informed, or correct than mine. And I have not been afraid to admit it.

We all learn from one another. And showing respect for your fellow board members, acknowledging their differences, and accepting their views as valid will undoubtedly strengthen one's position for a future date, as people tend to listen more carefully to someone they view as intelligent, well-informed, fair, and courteous. We get back what we give, and if we give others our unbiased attention and consideration, they are more likely to return the courtesy and perhaps change their vote to coincide with our own position on an important future issue.

2   Just What Do They Want from Me?

Now that you've left your hat at the door, and you understand the importance of impartiality and commitment to the board as discussed in chapter 1, you need to understand the principles behind board governance, and where you, as a director, fit into the scheme of things. What will your responsibilities (also referred to as "due diligence") be as a director on this board? What are your rights as a director? And what is fiduciary duty? We will address each of these questions in this chapter.

Essentially, the board is the governing body of an organization and is a continuous corporate entity. Members of the board will come and go, but the board will remain as the ultimate authority of any organization or association. The duties of the board are to manage the organization and oversee senior staff, such as the executive director. Staff are employees and operate under direction from the board.

You, as an individual director, will likely assume specific responsibilities for a portion of the organization's business and activities. As part of the board, you will help plan and implement the future path for the organization by becoming involved in the strategic planning and goal-setting of the group as a whole. You will also help manage the finances of the organization by developing the annual budget or approving the budget prepared by its staff. This is important stuff!

It is therefore your responsibility to find out as much as possible about the organization — whether you are just considering taking on a directorship or are already on the board.

Ethical Decision-making

Occasionally, while doing research on an organization, you may learn that it supports a cause or position you don't or can't ethically stand behind. It would therefore be your duty to decline the board position, as it is unlikely that you could fully support the organization's goals or projects.

Just what is ethics all about? For a detailed explanation, visit the website of Santa Clara University (California) at *www.scu.edu/ethics/practicing/decision/framework.html*. Here, you will find an excellent interpretation of all the considerations that apply to making ethical decisions. A basic summary suggests that ethics is not about science, religion, feelings, or simply following the law. Making ethical decisions is about doing the "right thing" with respect to:

⇨ creating an optimum balance of good over harm;

⇨ protecting and respecting moral rights; and

⇨ acting with virtue to the best of the human condition.

Bonnie Zink has extensive experience working in the healthcare/non-profit field in Saskatchewan, and helped put together a board manual for the Saskatchewan Association of Health Organizations (SAHO) in 2003. She is passionate about the issue of ethical decision-making: "As healthcare can be one of the most politicized issues of our day, ethical decision-making is an important component of every board-run organization."

She adds, "We need to ask ourselves questions such as: Who receives a piece of the very limited resources available? How much ought they be entitled to? Why will organization A be successful over organization B in lobbying for the desired outcome? These are questions that remain central to any board decision with respect to the allocation of funds and other resources."

Zink says that thinking and acting ethically as individual board members and as an organization will help ensure that each board decision is carefully deliberated and provides the fairest outcome possible. "Most healthcare boards are publicly funded, and decisions that determine where to allocate resources must be carefully thought out and validated in an ethical and transparent manner," says Zink. "Thus ethics is an integral part of the decision-making process that both new and veteran board members ought to consider."

For more on ethical decision-making, visit *character-counts.org*, where you can sign up for a free e-newsletter from the Josephson Institute, a U.S.-based organization that develops and delivers services and educational materials that aim to increase ethical commitment, competence, and practice in all segments of society. A variety of resources are also available for purchase, including a thirty-three-page booklet written by Michael Josephson called *Making Ethical Decisions.*

It is tremendously important to fully understand the background and backbone of the organization you will be serving. Conduct your research by reading published articles about the organization. Does it have a media clipping service? If so, get a hold of the archived articles. Or simply perform an Internet search for the organization. This will likely provide you with all you need to know — and more. You can also talk to members of the staff or seasoned directors, and read the organization's constitution, bylaws, or past minutes of the board. The more you learn about the organization, the more effective you will be as one of its new directors.

If you don't understand something you have come across in your research, ask for an explanation. If you are thorough in your research, you will set yourself up for success. Engaging in a hurried or uninformed decision will make saying yes the wrong thing to do — both for you and for the organization. It is your obligation and due diligence as a director to be well-informed and engaged in the issues affecting the organization. You can only do this if you immerse yourself in its business, become fully aware of its concerns, and attend meetings regularly.

Most boards are not simply looking for "bums to fill the seats," to use a popular expression. They are looking for individuals who care enough to educate themselves about the organization and to truly make a difference through their participation on the organization's driving force.

Understanding Fiduciary Duty

When discussing board governance, due diligence, and responsibilities of the board of directors, you will often hear the phrase "fiduciary duty." This means that you, as a director, must always act in the best interest of the organization.

We've already discussed how important it is for you to fulfill your due diligence by becoming highly knowledgeable about the organization you will be serving. In your fiduciary duty as a director, it is also important for you to act in the utmost of good faith, and be unquestionably honest and completely loyal to the organization.

Sounds a bit like we might be describing the family Fido, but I can assure you, the role of a director is not to be an obedient pet, but rather to be a leading force that will take the organization on to bigger and better things. Just as long as you remember that you are part of a team and must make all decisions *in the best interest of the organization as a whole* and not simply to make your life easier or to more quickly complete an assigned task.

I've sat on a board where a very well-meaning director acted without consultation and put the names of her fellow directors in a publication without getting their consent. It was clear that she meant well and that her intentions were good and honourable; however, it was her fiduciary duty to consult her fellow directors prior to proceeding with the action — even if she thought that her actions were correct and above reproach. Directors are part of a team and should never act unilaterally unless they have been given clear authority to do so.

Board Confidentiality

Board confidentiality is another important issue that warrants discussion. The trusty *Oxford Canadian Dictionary* defines *fiduciary* as "based in trust." When you are a director, it is your duty is to act in a most trustworthy fashion and hold board knowledge in trust and confidence until instructed to release it to the public, your constituents, or even someone as trusted (to you) as your spouse.

This can be very difficult. When you are on a board of directors, many people will come to you asking for information about what has been discussed at a meeting. You may have known them a long time. You may feel you can trust them. They will be very persuasive, and promise not to share the information with anyone else. But remember: now that you are a director, your first allegiance is to the board. Don't let yourself feel pressured into acting improperly or without careful thought.

To help you to prepare for such enquiries, before you leave a board meeting be sure that you clearly understand what information can be released if asked, when it can be released, and to whom.

Using Tip Sheets

On one board I belonged to, the issues were so complex that the organization prepared "tip sheets" for its directors. These useful documents provided directors with clear and correct information — accessible at their fingertips — so that answers given by the various board members to the inevitable questions were all accurate and along the same wavelength. This was extremely helpful, and a practice I would recommend to any board dealing with complex or sensitive issues.

Maureen Cavan, executive director of Access Copyright, leads the progressive organization I am speaking of, and has been responsible for introducing many positive changes that have helped to streamline the collective, resulting in a more effective board for her to work with.

"Clear speaking notes defining facts and reasoning for decisions taken by the board of directors are an invaluable tool for board members in maintaining open communications with the community they represent," says Cavan. "They ensure that all members of the community receive the same clear messages and they provide board members with the confidence to clearly present positions and answer questions."

Some people may feel that providing directors with speaking notes is a form of filtering or influencing what is being said. In some cases this may be true, but when you are dealing with complex issues that can be easily misunderstood, it is my opinion that providing directors with clear, comprehensive information only makes the directors, and ultimately the organization, stronger and more effective.

As directors, we generally take quickly written brief notes at meetings, but are they written in the same language (with the same tone and accuracy) as what might be written by informed staff following a long and intense meeting? Not likely.

Having expertly prepared notes or an executive summary distributed to all directors at, or immediately following, a meeting will eliminate uncertainty and the dissemination of inaccurate or inappropriate information. It will still enable you to put your own personal spin on the information — as long as you don't distort the facts.

The digital world has made it so easy for any organization to quickly forward an electronic document to all directors following a meeting. If this is done, there can be no excuse for directors to complain about insufficient time or information necessary to provide feedback or a report to their constituents following the meeting, as most of the work has already in effect been done for them!

What Are Your Rights?

We've now learned about the responsibilities of board members. But what are your rights as a director?

⇨ A director has the right to full and proper training in addition to a copy of the board manual containing constitution and bylaws, etc. This topic is covered in more detail in chapter 4.

⇨ A director has the right to full disclosure. Before you are asked to vote on an issue, make sure you have all the facts so that you can make an informed and enlightened decision. Occasionally, staff may be busy with other tasks or not see the importance of your request. Make it clear that you need the information (and by when), but be polite and considerate in your actions.

⇨ A director has the right to a safe and secure environment in which to conduct meetings. If you feel the location of board meetings or board accommodations is unsafe or undesirable, let the rest of the board and the key staff members know how you feel. Ask that an appropriate alternative location be considered. Be reasonable in your request and in considering the alternatives.

⇨ A director has the right to insist that improvements be made to the premises to correct unsafe conditions. If you notice that a railing is broken or missing, insist that it be fixed. If you notice that a slip and fall situation repeatedly exists at the premises of the association, insist that it be remedied, as directors may be held personally liable in the case of a lawsuit.

⇨   A director has the right to insist the organization engage outside help if the board or staff does not possess the time or expertise to address a certain issue or task. The use of external experts is quite common. Boards often hire lawyers, accountants, bookkeepers, tax professionals, and other experts to help them more efficiently and effectively deal with a situation.

⇨   A director has the right to insist that the organization carry sufficient general liability and directors and officer insurance to ensure that the organization and its directors are indemnified against risk. (See more on this topic in chapter 5.)

Now that you understand your rights and responsibilities as a director, you are ready to learn more about the different types of boards and how to run effective meetings.

3

What Kind of Board Is This?

In chapter 2, we talked about how boards are governed and about your fiduciary duty as a director. We are now going to take a close look at the different styles in which boards are operated, as well as at board etiquette and the tools that boards use to operate efficiently and effectively.

Styles of Board Governance

There are several different styles of boards, and over the years I have sat on a variety of boards that reflect most of these. There is a more complex explanation — which we will later address — but for a beginning director, the most important consideration is how you as an individual director will fit into the pie and how big your piece of pie will be.

Some boards are very hands-on and often referred to as "working" boards. In this type of environment, directors are expected to engage in tasks that would normally or ideally be done by staff. That means you will be responsible for a fairly large piece of the organizational pie.

Other boards operate under a management-style of authority and are referred to as "advisory" boards. In this type of environment, the board prefers only to oversee and direct activity, as opposed to actually being involved in day-to-day tasks. Your piece of the organizational pie (or direct responsibility for getting things done) will be smaller and less time-consuming.

Then there are boards that are a combination of both, asking directors to work on complex or high-profile projects with staff handling most of the regular operations and providing support to the board as required.

The type of board it is will provide a clear indication of how much of your time will be involved. Before you say yes, be sure to ask the following questions:

⇨ **What type of board is this?** (Is it a working, hands-on board?)

⇨ **How many paid staff does the organization have?** (If it is two or less, you can be sure the board leans more toward the hands-on camp.)

⇨ **How much of your time is required in order to fulfill your obligations?** (Will you be asked to chair a committee? Will you be responsible for organizing a special event?)

Getting straight answers to these questions may not always be easy. Talk to previous and current directors and compare their answers. Is there some consistency?

If not, dig deeper, talk to more people. Know what you will be up against — before you say yes.

Do not make the decision with haste and do not let anyone pressure you into making your decision without having the answers to the above questions. You need to know, up front, exactly what type of board you're dealing with and what will be expected of you. Anyone who responds to your queries with a "Don't worry about it" is being unfair to you and preventing you from making a fully informed decision.

You will most often find non-profit charitable boards to be of the hands-on type. That is because these organizations generally operate within very tight budgets and cannot afford large staffs. Therefore, many of the tasks deemed important by the board will have to be done by volunteers — board members and others delegated by the board to serve on committees or task forces.

Be aware that if you agree to sit on this type of board, your time commitment is likely to be extensive, as you are not just a figurehead leader of the organization; you are certain to be asked to chair a committee and get jobs done — whether by doing them yourself or with the help of other volunteers. You may also be responsible for recruiting those volunteers to help you. Subsequently, the time commitment is likely to be considerable.

Of course, everyone's lifestyle is different, and a three hour per week time commitment may seem quite reasonable to an individual who does not have full-time employment or who is not already engaged in a myriad of other activities. Whereas, someone with small children, a full-time job, chronic illness in the family, or other constraints on his or her time may find three hours per week to be a formidable volunteer commitment. One size definitely does not fit all, and it's strongly recommended to ensure that the board's style is a custom fit to your individual situation.

If time is an issue for you, a board that practises the management or advisory style of operations will be more suitable for you, as it is less likely to interfere with your other commitments. Mid-sized non-profit organizations with ten to twenty staff usually have a blended style: less hands-on than their smaller sisters, but more hands-on than larger non-profits with a staff greater than twenty.

You may come across additional terms for board styles. Bruce Wilson, vice-president of the Professional Writers Association of Canada (PWAC), has found studying the Garber Models of Governance to be of great help to his association. After many years of organizational growth and change, the PWAC board has evolved to operate as a "Policy Board" in which the board:

- ⇨ establishes guiding principles;
- ⇨ delegates responsibility and authority; and
- ⇨ monitors compliance to ensure staff and the board are on the same wavelength.

Garber's model also includes descriptions of the advisory board, the patron board, the cooperative board, and the management team board. See *garberconsulting.com* for a full explanation of the Garber Models of Governance.

Wilson has also studied John Carver's philosophy on board governance and highly recommends a five-star rated book called *Boards that Make a Difference* written by John Carver and published by Wiley & Sons. See the box below for Wilson's review of the book. Visit *www.policygovernance.com* for more on Carver's Policy Governance ® Model.

Boards that Make a Difference: A New Design for Leadership in Nonprofit and Public Organizations by John Carver. Second edition, 1997, Wiley & Sons.

A Review by Bruce Wilson

John Carver is the well-known creator of Policy Governance, a popular system of board governance used by profit and non-profit boards around the world. In *Boards that Make a Difference*, Carver outlines the principles of Policy Governance as applied to non-profit organizations and describes four basic categories: the governing board, the advisory board, the line board, and the workgroup board.

The book focuses on the governing board and assumes that as the optimal model for non-profits. For organizations that use the popular "working board" model, where the board is involved in the day-to-day management of operations, Carver's book offers little advice. However, many working boards have successfully incorporated the features of policy governance while staying involved in management functions, so a hybridized model is not only possible, but often desirable in some organizations.

The "meat" of the book is in defining the complex relationship between the board and the CEO (or executive director). The CEO is responsible for managing the staff and the board should give the CEO complete freedom in determining how that is done. The board should not meddle in the tasks assigned to the CEO, nor should they look over his or her shoulder to see how they are being accomplished. In Carver's terminology, the board should be concerned with "ends" — i.e. results, impacts, goals, and outcomes — while the CEO is concerned with "means" — the nuts and bolts process of achieving ends.

Carver includes useful chapters on clarifying and sustaining an organization's mission, the board–executive relationship, board self-management, the role of committees and officers, standards of ethics and prudence, the levels of policy development, and efficient meetings.

Organizations with a highly active membership and a strong sense of ownership, such as many professional groups, need a clear mechanism by which members interact with the board and staff without getting in the way. Carver does discuss the need for "linkage" between board and owners, but gives it only a slight treatment. The book would have been much stronger had Carver included an entire chapter to organizations with high involvement from owners. This is NOT a book for organizations that use a direct democracy model of governance, where members must be consulted on all issues and majority decisions made before going forward!

Overall, *Boards that Make a Difference* is an essential reference for all non-profit boards, and for Carver purists, provides the best guide for applying his Policy Governance model to non-profits.

How Formal Is the Board?

We've given you quite a few options to think about when it comes to board governance. Another important consideration regarding the style of the board is its formality and etiquette.

Some boards are quite formal and operate strictly under a pre-determined protocol such as Robert's Rules of Order in which all or most discussion is tied to the making of motions (that formalize and record board business). If this is the case on the board you are considering, be aware that idle chatter is likely not permitted or is very limited. This would therefore not be the best match for a stay-at-home mom who is joining a board to get out and talk with adults, or retired individuals with plenty of time on their hands and the desire for unrestricted conversation. The more formal structure would, however, be well suited to someone with very limited time, as he or she would know that their time will be well-spent and not "wasted" on unrelated conversation.

The same concern may apply to formality of dress. Some boards require that directors attend meetings in business attire. Others are completely informal and anything goes. Find out ahead to avoid embarrassment and unexpected costs that may be associated with buying the "right clothes."

Board Etiquette

John (Jay) H. Remer Jr. is a North American consultant specializing in corporate etiquette and international protocol. He writes regularly about etiquette on his website *www.etiquetteguy.com* and has extensive cross-border board experience on which he reflects. "Sitting on a corporate board is different than a non-profit board, but still formal," says Remer. "You should dress appropriately, learn to adhere to Robert's Rules of Order — and leave your egos at home."

Remer says that a lot of people have ego problems that they don't want to address. "There are definitely personality types that are not well-suited to serving on boards, as they are not team players. Leaders have to keep those personalities in check and refrain ... from disrupting the focus of the team." He also says there are three categories of board responsibilities that potential candidates should be aware of. You may be asked to:

⇨ give or get money (i.e. engage in fundraising for the organization);
⇨ give your time; or
⇨ share expertise that stems from your own practical experience.

"In order to be an effective board member, you must fit at least two of those criteria," says Remer. "And remember, misleading other people is very disrespectful and that is definitely bad etiquette."

Board etiquette is a very important consideration and one that should be taken seriously by any board member. When you attend a board meeting, be fully in attendance — in body, mind, and spirit. That means no texting, checking email or tweeting on your cell phone or laptop, or engaging in any other distracting activity unless it is specific to the effective functioning of the meeting and you are doing so for clarification on an issue or to get the word out quickly about something relevant to board business.

I was once on a board on which two directors brought their knitting needles and were knitting during the board meetings. It was very disruptive to the flow of the meetings as you could see two sets of knitting needles moving out of the corner of your eye and hear them clicking from time to time. Other directors and the staff must have experienced the same distracting effects, as the two directors were quickly asked to refrain from knitting at the board table.

This comment was made not to belittle the efforts of the directors, as both are great gals and worked hard on behalf of the organization, but I do agree that when directors are sitting at the board table, their complete attention should be on board business and not partially diverted to a non-essential pastime.

As an effective director you first must be true to yourself, as only you can accurately assess your own qualifications and only you can stand up to the commitment you will make as a board member. You then must be true to others and do your very best to meet any expectations

By engaging in an activity that takes your attention away from board business during meetings, you are sending a message that says one of the following things:

⇨ I am so smart that I don't need to fully concentrate on what is being said.

⇨ I'm not really interested in what you are saying.

⇨ I really don't want to be here.

⇨ Other things are more important to me than being on this board.

Are these messages that you want to give to your fellow board members or the staff of the organization?

you have created regarding your abilities and commitment to the organization. That means giving your complete attention to what's going on from the beginning to the very end of each meeting.

Understanding Robert's Rules of Order

Robert's Rules of Order (RRO) are most commonly defined as the widely accepted set of rules and guidelines used to administer productive and orderly meetings and conventions. Originally developed in 1876 by an American military man, General Henry Martyn Robert, RRO have been greatly revised over the past two hundred plus years and have been adopted by the vast majority of North American non-profit organizations.

Anyone taking on a board position in Canada or the United States should become familiar with RRO and learn how to use them.

In a nutshell, RRO provide a template that helps organizations run predictable meetings according to a pre-set agenda that might look something like this:

Essential Components to a Board/Business Meeting

- ✓ Motion to adopt agenda as presented (moved and seconded).
- ✓ Are there any amendments (additions) to the agenda? (Amendments must be moved and seconded.)
- ✓ Motion to adopt minutes from previous meeting (moved and seconded).
- ✓ Are there any errors or omissions (corrections) to those minutes?
- ✓ Is there any business arising from the minutes?
- ✓ Committee and/or Executive reports.
- ✓ Old/Unfinished Business.
- ✓ New Business/Announcements.
- ✓ Motion to Adjourn (moved, seconded, and non-debatable).

If you make a motion, you will be the first one permitted to speak in support of the motion, followed by the individual who seconded your motion. Discussion by all will follow and you will be the last person permitted to speak before the vote is cast. When the vote is called for, you must either vote in favour, against, or abstain (refrain) from voting in a case where for some reason you are confused or not clearly for or against the issue being discussed. Every motion is debatable (open for discussion) except for the motion to adjourn. The chair can delay the motion to adjourn if there is important unfinished business that must be handled on the day of the meeting.

That's RRO in brief and simplified terms. There is much more detail to be understood, but that is beyond the scope of this book. This book is intended only to give current and prospective directors the tools they need to attend a meeting without being completely in the dark as to protocol and expectations followed by the majority of non-profit associations and organizations in Canada and the United States.

Roger Woloshyn is an expert on Canadian Parliamentary Law, a Distinguished Toastmaster, and a member of the Manitoba Association of Parliamentarians. He is also a strong supporter of the importance of Robert's Rules of Order and running meetings according to the book.

"I know of a non-profit association that approved a $40,000 expenditure towards a building project and then found that the meeting at which the motion had been passed did not have quorum (the number of directors or voters required to make it an 'official' meeting.) The motion was therefore void and the whole mess ended up delaying the project and would have made the board liable for damages had the organization not been adequately covered with proper insurance," cautions Woloshyn. He says that every director must become intimately familiar with RRO. "You don't ever go into the game without knowing the rules. And you have to be sure that someone doesn't try and change the rules midstream — because their agenda may not be the same as the board's."

To learn the rules without having to get too technical, Woloshyn recommends the book *Robert's Rules of Order, Newly Revised — In Brief* written by the Council of the Robert's Rules Association. It can be purchased online from the official RRO site at *www.robertsrules.com*. If you are looking for a more in-depth account of RRO, Woloshyn recommends what he calls the best book of its kind, *Parliamentary Law,* published in 1923 by Henry M. Robert himself as an update to his earlier work on RRO.

Roger's Quick and Simple Guide to RRO

We use Robert's Rules of Order so that:

⇨ we discuss one thing at a time.

⇨ one person speaks at a time.

⇨ there is only one motion on the same issue per meeting.

⇨ everyone has a fair and equal opportunity to speak.

⇨ there are enough people present to make an informed decision.

⇨ the rights of *all* members are protected.

⇨ majority rules.

⇨ we avoid chaos.

⇨ we don't waste time and human resources.

Experts like Woloshyn have some solid advice for boards: "If you do not feel confident that you or anyone on the board can chair an important meeting properly, use a parliamentarian. And for anyone wanting to learn how to handle a meeting the easy way, join a Toastmasters club or a Parliamentary club with a view to learn Robert's Rules and, more importantly, how to chair a meeting. This skill is acquired only by doing — there is no other way!"

4

Help!

In this chapter, we'll discuss the importance of board training and the need for a thorough and proper orientation for all new board members.

Orientation and Training

I have been on many boards and found there to be vast differences in the levels of effort and professionalism put into preparing new directors for the important role they are about to fill. Some organizations put a massive effort into providing new directors with full kits containing a complete list of motions passed within the past year, the organization's mission and vision statements, its code of ethics, and other information about the organization's history, mantras, and raison d'être.

Being inundated with all this information may be somewhat overwhelming, but I can assure you that too much is far better than not enough. You can learn to quickly sift through the myriad of information before you and retain what is most important to your own individual role on the board.

Other organizations are woefully lacking with respect to board orientation, and prefer the "sink or swim" approach to director training. It is imperative to quickly find out the type of organization you are dealing with. If they don't have sufficient training for your needs, you can either improvise and find a current or former director to give you guidance, insist that the organization formally provide you with this information, or walk away from the opportunity/invitation to serve on the board.

Receiving proper training without having to ask for it is obviously the preferred route, as it leaves no doubt about what you are getting into. An organization with a thorough and well-planned director's orientation and training program is a blessing and a recipe for success. In cases where no such training program is in place, you may want to find someone in the organization who you admire and trust and ask them to mentor you. If this is not an option then the last acceptable option is to *ask* the organization for training and sufficient background documentation. Perhaps no one has inquired about an orientation/training program previously and the organization doesn't realize its importance or that its system may be missing an integral component.

That exact scenario occurred at an organization at which I once volunteered. Director's training had been rather limited and after my asking for more, they did set up a more comprehensive training program — now one of the best I have come across. This progressive organization now provides new directors with a complete binder containing all the pertinent information one needs to know. They also provide a full day of on-site orientation to quickly familiarize new directors with key aspects of the operation, and provide ongoing board training for all directors at the in-person quarterly board meetings. I venture to say it doesn't get any better than that.

The needs of every organization will be different. Small, community-based associations or clubs will not likely have formal training or an extensive assortment of resource material for board members. They may not have the human or financial resources to do so, or perhaps no one has ever asked about it. But every organization — large or small — should at least offer each new board member a copy of their constitution (every non-profit in Canada should have one) containing the goals and objectives of the organization, information concerning vacancies on the board, and provisions for membership and board meetings.

Even the recreation club in the tiny community in which I live provided me with this information when I joined its board. I was surprised and overjoyed to see that even small, rural organizations can be as efficient and professionally run as their big-city counterparts — sometimes more so. Just remember, it's one thing to be given information, but it's your responsibility to make proper use of it. Be sure to read the documentation you are given, as it will provide you with the tools to more competently do your job as director.

Trade unions are very adept at training their volunteers. Some of the best training I have ever received in leadership, negotiating, and volunteer recruitment came from my union days. So, hats off to our brothers and sisters in the labour movement for taking care of their own, which in turn reflects favourably on the organization, its membership, and often the community at large. The good thing about local unions is that they are usually connected to larger parent unions with bigger budgets and greater access to training for their volunteers. The key thing is to remember to take advantage of all this free training and let it work for you.

You may not realize it at the time, but the training that you receive — whether it is focused on leadership, communication, or other life-skills — is very likely to be transferable and useful in other aspects of your life and career.

I have certainly found this to be true. The incredibly comprehensive training I received as a leader within my component of the Manitoba Government Employees Union back in the 1980s continues to be useful to me today.

As you take on the challenges of each new role, you take all the knowledge, training, and experience gained from the previous role with you. This enhanced knowledge makes you better in each subsequent role you take on as you journey along your life path. We continue to grow as we continue to learn.

Yes, there will be people who come to the board table suggesting that something needs to be changed because they did it better or differently when they were on another board. Sometimes we need to simply and politely thank them for their input and move on. And sometimes we should take heed and listen to what they are saying and realize that there is indeed often a better way to do things.

Performance Evaluations

We can never be *too* good at anything, so something to consider as a new director of any given board is whether your performance will be formally assessed or evaluated. If so, welcome the challenge and opportunity for improvement, as it will help you continue to grow in your role — and as a person.

On one board I served on, we evaluated every aspect of board relations. This included:

⇨ self-assessment (you evaluate your own participation and understanding of board matters);

⇨ peer assessment (directors anonymously evaluate one another);

⇨ leader assessment (directors evaluate the board's chair[s]); and

⇨ board interaction with key staff (such as the executive director).

The results of these assessments should be carefully tabulated and compared (i.e., your assessment of your own performance should be compared to how others on the board assessed you). As a director trying to do the best job I could, I found this information to be quite valuable as it helped me focus on areas that could use some improvement. It also made me realize that I was doing a pretty darn good job. It also provided the organization with a formal mechanism by which directors not fulfilling their roles or responsibilities could be coached, further encouraged, and, if necessary, asked to leave the board or informed that they should not seek re-election. Board evaluations are likely to get more buy-in and cooperation from all parties if they are not perceived as punitive — meaning not intended to punish, create embarrassment, or be of a "finger pointing" nature. But it is also important for all parties concerned to believe that the evaluations are meaningful and will be acted upon if results warrant that some form of corrective action be taken.

An organization with which I am intimately familiar once had trouble with a director who didn't attend meetings, and when he did, was always leaving the room for "smoke breaks." He also reportedly drank too much and was not an effective contributor to the board. Some said he was taking up space, and not providing enough value by way of his service in return. This director was asked to resign from the board but would not do so willingly before his term was up. If that organization had a board evaluation system in place, there would have been a mechanism by which that director's performance would have been evaluated and the director possibly forced to resign if corrective action wasn't taken when his shortcomings were addressed.

I have also been on a board where more than one director did not attend meetings regularly. This was not fair to the directors who did attend regularly as they ended up having to take on more work than they bargained for when they took on a director's position.

In my opinion, being subject to board evaluations is a good thing, as it increases the accountability of each and every director and of the board as a whole.

Now let's look at it from an organization's point of view. As executive director of Access Copyright, Maureen Cavan's constituents are governments, educational institutions, and other users of copyrighted materials, as well as the publishers and creators who have produced that material. She reports to an eighteen-member board comprised of various members of these communities. "I believe board evaluation is a necessary and valuable tool to ensure board members fully understand their individual responsibilities to the organization and to each other," says Cavan. "How each board goes about doing this is very dependent on the size and make-up of the board itself. It is more difficult to do peer assessments on a large board where members see each other only occasionally and may not work together on committees. The most valuable tools, in my opinion, are those that measure overall board functioning and self-assessment as a board participant."

Cavan believes that self-assessment forces each director to take personal stock of his or her contribution to the responsibilities held by the board of directors and that sharing this self assessment with the chair of the board also allows for performance evaluation — an important part of any role that carries responsibility.

Since her organization has introduced a formal board evaluation system, Cavan has seen less effective board members decide not to stand for re-election when their terms were up, resulting in a more effective board comprised of individuals who may be more passionate about the issues and have sufficient time to embrace them. She says, "I think a board that practices self-assessment becomes more conscious of the important role held by each member individually. This, in turn, leads to an increased effort to become and remain more aware of the issues and challenges faced by the organization they are charged with leading."

Points You Might Be Evaluated On in Your Role as Director

⇨ Attendance and promptness at meetings.

⇨ Effectively contributing to discussions at meetings.

⇨ Being prepared for meetings (reading/doing your homework).

⇨ Willingness to take on roles and duties.

⇨ Willingness to help others (mentoring).

⇨ Interacting well with fellow directors and staff.

⇨ Ability to think independently and without bias.

⇨ Demonstrating sound judgment.

⇨ Being consultative or a team player in nature.

⇨ Being knowledgeable of the organization's issues.

5

Limit Your Exposure

Directors and Officers Insurance

It's surprising how many current and potential directors do not realize the importance of Directors and Officers (D&O) insurance. The right type of comprehensive D&O insurance is absolutely imperative to the operations of any not-for-profit board, especially in today's world, where people sue or attempt to sue for just about anything.

If the organization soliciting your participation does not have D&O coverage in place, I highly recommend that you *not* say yes until such a policy is in place. And ask to see the D&O policy when it has been put into effect, just to be sure that good intentions have been followed through to fruition and that you understand the provisions of coverage.

Many people will try and minimize the importance of this type of insurance, saying there is no risk on their type of board or that their board is indemnified through its by-laws and that is sufficient. But don't listen! There is a risk on virtually any board. I have seen a serious threat of at least four lawsuits against various boards I have worked with over the past twenty-five plus years. Without proper D&O insurance, the individual directors of a board could be at risk of financial loss if they have also been named in any lawsuit filed against the organization they are governing. After all, the board determines policy for the organization, and the directors are therefore responsible for the actions of the board.

Without proper D&O insurance, if a lawsuit was filed against the organization you are representing *and* its board, your personal assets *could* be at risk if you are found to be liable. This is a drastic example, but to make a point, how would you like to lose your house as a result of a wrongful dismissal lawsuit filed against the organization by a bitter former employee? It can happen — if the organization does not have proper D&O insurance in place to protect its directors against such situations.

Questions to Ask

Industry Canada has some tremendously useful information on its website at *www.ic.gc.ca* that will help a prospective director understand more about not-for-profit law and how it applies to non-profit and charitable organizations.

They list a number of questions on page 13 in chapter 6 of the *Primer for Directors of Non-Profit Corporations* that prospective and current directors should be asking their organizations:

⇨ Are the organization's policies recorded in written form and distributed to all board members?

⇨ Has the organization conducted a recent audit of its legal risks? When and by whom?

⇨ Do the organization's bylaws indemnify its directors?

⇨ Does the organization inform its directors about legal issues and protect them from any possible litigation?

⇨ Does the organization frequently deal with children or other vulnerable persons? Is there a formal screening policy for directors and those with authority?

⇨ Does the organization have a formal policy dealing with sexual abuse?

⇨ Does the organization have sufficient insurance to cover potential liability? How often is the insurance coverage reviewed and by whom?

⇨ Does the organization have directors and officers liability insurance for its directors, officers and key staff? What exactly does it cover?

Then ask yourself ...

⇨ Have I read the association's policies? Do I understand them?

⇨ Do I understand the legal risks facing the association and facing me as a director of this association?

⇨ Am I am satisfied that the association's screening practices are appropriate?

⇨ Do I understand the insurance coverage that is in place?

These questions have been reproduced with the permission of the Minister of Public Works and Government Services, 2009.

We all like to think that we will never be involved in a lawsuit (or be involved in one through the association we are associated with), just as we hope we will never experience a house fire — but we should still buy fire insurance.

Having worked in the insurance industry for eighteen years, I know the importance of insurance and how little value the average person places on it — until they have a claim. They soon learn that it was a very bad idea to scrimp on their insurance coverage. The same goes for boards. I've been on various association boards and have heard fellow directors or staff of the organization say "We can't really afford that" when discussing the financial impact of the proposed premium for a D&O policy.

The coverage is affordable, but not cheap, and is dependent on the asset size of the organization. For example, it would likely cost between six hundred and a thousand dollars a year for coverage for a small recreation club or sports association with a small budget, one hundred members, ten directors, and no staff. The D&O coverage for a non-profit professional association with a larger budget, five hundred members, ten directors, and two staff members is more likely to be in the range of fifteen hundred dollars per year.

"Although some companies might, we don't specifically determine a rate based on the number of directors or officers," says Mark Reszel, senior vice-president of D&O Liability at the Ottawa-based Encon Group Inc., one of Canada's major providers of D&O insurance and a specialist in non-profit coverage. "Total number of employees is a rating factor, but it's not our starting point," says Reszel, who goes on to say that Encon begins its analysis by looking at the size of the organization's assets and revenues, and then reviews its financial health, claims history, bylaws, jurisdiction in which the association operates (i.e. national or local), and its specific operations to rate its D&O policies.

"A service club would benefit from a lower rate than a disciplinary or licensing body due to its lower relative loss exposure," says Reszel. "So it's very important for the client to sit down with their broker and deal with the specifics of the organization's operations in order to get the policy customized for their needs." Reszel suggests that dealing with a broker who has extensive D&O experience is advantageous to the insured. "It's such an evolving area, and policy wordings and coverages are constantly changing," he says.

In his role as head of D&O underwriting at Encon, Reszel needs to know the differences between his company's policies and that of other insurers. He feels it's up to the insurance-buying public to be sure they understand the differences between policies as well. "The number one misconception is that all D&O policies are the same, and that's definitely not the case, so clients should not just go by the price of the policy. They need to understand what is and is not covered by each policy."

This is good, solid advice coming from someone who really understands the complexities of the business and the importance of obtaining the correct coverage. Without the right coverage, consider the cost of rebuilding your association in the event of an uninsured claim — or rebuilding your life, in the event that you become party to a suit. So be sure to make the choice that is right for your association, and to stick to your guns if you receive opposition on the issue. No board can truly afford to be without proper D&O insurance unless it has very considerable liquid assets and can afford to self-insure against such risks.

Having worked a long time in the insurance industry, I am fortunate to have access to a comprehensive assortment of resources in the insurance industry, but because Directors and Officers insurance is a rather complex subject, to deepen my understanding I turned to Peter Harper. Harper is a well-known and highly regarded insurance consultant with forty years experience, who gives independent insurance advice to non-profits, governments, and businesses through his two companies. If you are in a position tasked with looking for D&O coverage for your board, I recommend visiting Harper's website at *www.harperrisk. com* for detailed information on this complex subject.

Harper confirms there are many different providers of D&O insurance and it is important for organizations to find the one that best suits their needs. That's where his services as an independent consultant come in and are worth exploring if your organization is very large, complex, or has needs far different than the norm. "Clients often ask why they need to buy this additional insurance when they are likely already indemnified by the organization's bylaws," says Harper. "The answer is that even though you may sometimes be indemnified or covered, the organization will be out of pocket. It is good governance to purchase D&O insurance and protect your organization from depleting its assets to indemnify its directors, officers and employees."

Harper also reminds us that even though the organization you represent may not be found responsible for any claim brought against it, if the organization is sued, it needs to defend itself and pay the legal defence costs — which can be considerable. As D&O insurance covers the defence costs associated with a claim, it makes good sense to have your bases covered and purchase a D&O policy.

Who and What Is Covered?

The first thing to understand is that D&O insurance is intended to cover purely financial losses. The organization's Comprehensive General Liability Policy (CGL) will provide coverage for losses resulting from bodily injury or property damage caused by a negligent act, and the Fire or All Perils Policy will cover other direct damage losses.

When applying for D&O insurance, your organization will be asked to complete an annual application in which the number of directors and officers of the organization must be named and their background and experience noted. For example, if you are a director of an organization applying for D&O insurance, you may be asked whether you have recently been involved in a bankruptcy, insolvency, or legal action specifically against the organization or any of its directors. It is important to answer all questions asked of you honestly and completely, for if the organization submits an application containing false information, the coverage for the entire organization could be voided.

As well, if any of your personal information or the crucial information of the organization changes during the year, it is important to notify your agent or the insurance provider of the D&O coverage in order to avoid having a claim denied on the basis of "material change of risk." If there has been a change mid-term, whether it applies to those named on the policy, to the operational activities of the organization, or to the financial stability of the organization, inform the insurance provider immediately.

D&O coverage should cover the organization's staff, the signing officers of the corporation (the secretary, treasurer, and president or CEO), the board of directors, and its committees and subsidiaries (formalized subgroups of the organization). It should be noted that claims against the D&O policy may originate from several sources. An outside party can sue the organization and its directors. Employees and volunteers (who are considered insiders) can sue the organization, its officers, and directors. Even the organization's directors and officers can sue any of the other parties covered by the policy.

"The most common type of non-profit D&O claims we see are those relating to employment practices liability," says Lynn Lindsay, vice-president of claims for Encon. "Employment issues such as wrongful dismissal and discrimination often come up in the context of D&O claims. When both allegations are present, the claim will often involve civil litigation with respect to the wrongful dismissal aspect of the claim, and referral to the Human Rights Commission with respect to the discrimination aspect of the claim. The D&O policy would pay for the defence of both actions."

It is important to understand that certain risks can't be transferred to insurance, such as the employer's (organization's) contractual obligations for the payment of wages. However, the defence cost coverage for wrongful dismissal claims can be of significant consequence to non-profit organizations. "Although you can't transfer risks that would be the employer's responsibility, the D&O policy would cover the defence costs, which can often be considerable — particularly to the smaller non-profit corporations who often do not have very large operating budgets," says Lindsay.

She also notes that this type of protection provides the greatest benefit to small non-profit associations and helps organizations be prepared for unexpected expenses resulting from litigation. Whether or not your organization is guilty of the allegations made against it does not eliminate the likelihood of being faced with considerable legal fees in the event a claim is advanced.

There are many misconceptions that individuals and organizations have about D&O insurance. Most often

Types of Claims or Unintentional Wrongful Acts That May Be Covered by D&O Insurance for Non-profits

✓   Allegations by staff with respect to wrongful dismissal, sexual harassment, or discrimination.
✓   Non-delivery of service to members or beneficiaries.
✓   Breach of trust on the part of a director.
✓   Non-payment of taxes to the government.
✓   Defamation.

* Misappropriation of funds, fraud, and embezzlement are occasionally covered, but it is harder to get coverage for these acts.

it is perceived by organizations that they already have all their insurance needs covered if they have separate physical damage (from fire, wind, etc.), crime, and liability coverage in place.

But that is not the case, for as we have noted, every Comprehensive General Liability (CGL) insurance policy, every physical damage policy, and every D&O policy will have exclusions and limitations. D&O insurance is intended to protect individuals from exposure related to the errors, omissions, or negligent acts of the directors and officers during the course of carrying out their duties for the organization. But even the comprehensive D&O insurance does not cover a breach of contractual obligations such as the obligation to pay wages or amounts owing to other creditors.

That said, it is still a very integral part of the insurance portfolio of any organization. "We try to explain to clients that insurance coverage is like a puzzle," says Lindsay. "You need to put all the pieces into the puzzle in order to have complete insurance coverage. That's why it's important for organizations to talk to their brokers, determine exactly what their risk exposures are and what insurance products are available to provide the necessary protection against those exposures."

Sample D&O Claims

Encon was kind enough to provide me with a few samples of D&O claims that they have authorized me to use in this book. Here are a few scenarios that unsuspecting non-profits may face:

Breach of Trust

The insured non-profit organization held a fundraising event during a festival run by another party. A float was advanced to the insured to be repaid out of the funds raised. The $200,000.00 float was deposited into the insured's bank account and subsequently could not be accounted for. A year after the claim was filed, the organization went bankrupt. Defence counsel was retained and the claim was ultimately resolved with a total of $30,000.00 in defence costs and $75,000.00 indemnity being paid.

Breach of Duty, Abuse of Process

The board of a professional association revoked the membership of a member due to allegations of unethical conduct. The member brought an action for damages in the amount of $350,000.00. She alleged the board of directors had targeted her, and that the bylaws of the association were not properly followed at the time of her expulsion. Defence counsel was retained and the claim was resolved by settlement with a total of $100,000.00 defence costs and an additional indemnity of $95,000.00 being paid.

Appeal of Wrongful Dismissal Suit

An organization terminated the employment of a senior executive after receiving complaints from other employees with respect to the executive's behaviour, which included alleged sexual misconduct and harassment of other employees. The dismissed executive sued the organization for wrongful termination and the directors for interference with contractual relations. The dismissed executive was successful at trial. The decision was successfully appealed. The executive's attempt to appeal to the Supreme Court was denied. There was a whopping total of $254,000.00 in defence costs paid by the D&O policy.

Wrongful Dismissal and Defamation

The executive director of a large non-profit was dismissed following a reorganization of operations and responsibilities. While the executive director had been dismissed with cause, the association had issued a slanderous letter about him to various third parties. The former ED brought an action claiming damages for pay in lieu of notice, defamation, vacation pay, loss of benefits, and punitive damages. Defence counsel was retained and the claim was resolved with a total of $55,000.00 in defence costs and a negotiated settlement of $110,000.00 being paid.

Misrepresentation, Breach of Fiduciary Duty

A foundation was established for the purpose of organizing a particular event. The foundation received a grant from the federal government to help finance the event. After the event took place, it was discovered that the foundation had incurred expenses in excess of its revenues. The government investigated and concluded that the grant monies had been used for purposes other than what had been represented. The government brought a claim against the directors and officers for damages arising as a result of the misrepresentations made regarding the use of funds and breach of fiduciary duty. Defence counsel was retained and the claim was resolved with a total of $35,000.00 in defence costs and a negotiated settlement of $120,000.00 being paid.

Professional Association Sued by a Member

A member of a professional association brought action against the association and several of its directors and officers over a disagreement with respect to licensing requirements. The member claimed damages for breach of fiduciary duty, defamation, and interference with economic interests. Defence counsel was retained and the claim was resolved with a total of $110,000.00 defence costs and a nominal settlement was paid.

These are just a few real-life examples of claims filed against non-profit boards and their directors. Hopefully, they have helped you better understand the importance of D&O insurance for non-profit associations and organizations. For a more complete list of claims examples, visit this link: *www.encon.ca/English/resources/ClaimsExamples/Pages/NonProfitOrganzations.aspx.*

Your organization's insurance broker can likely help the board with clarification and completion of the application. But if you are seeking a greater understanding of D&O insurance on your own, you can also look to the following well-respected independent groups for guidance: Volunteer Canada (*volunteer.ca/volcan/eng/content/board/program.php*); The Nonprofit Risk Management Center (*www.nonprofitrisk.org*); and Imagine Canada (*www.imaginecanada.ca*).

All of these organizations have an abundance of useful information on their websites.

6 Are You Ready?

"Disaster Plans"

We have learned about Robert's Rules of Order, board governance, the fiduciary duty of a director, board training, and the various types of boards we may encounter. We have also talked about the necessary insurance that boards require in order to protect their directors from unforeseen situations. But what if, even after all the proper precautions have been taken, the board finds itself facing a disaster of unimaginable measures? This happened to an organization I was serving quite some years ago and the horror still lingers with each director who was on that board at the time.

The situation was that we had one key staff member quit in a fury. This person was thereby unwilling to share knowledge about the organization contained in her head and removed precious files to which we could no longer gain access. Immediately following this unfortunate event, the sole remaining staff person quit

in protest of our perceived mishandling of the situation
and our national five-hundred-member organization
was left without any staff to serve it. We were facing a
disastrous situation without any plan of action — and
without access to our national office and all the essential information it contained about our organizational
history and operations. What could we have done differently to have better dealt with, or perhaps prevented,
the unfortunate situation entirely?

Establishing an Executive Committee

"There is no way a board can anticipate that an individual will behave in an extreme or irrational manner," says
Otto Siebenmann, a Toronto-based barrister and solici-
tor who has been practising law for nearly thirty years
and has valuable experience guiding numerous charitable and non-profit associations. "My best advice to
non-profit organizations would be for them to have an
executive committee of at least three people — prefer-
ably in the same city as the organization's national office
— who could react to a situation and make decisions
and take quick action without first having to consult
with the entire board."

Siebenmann says the entire board should define
what authority it will designate to its executive committee and that should then be stated in the organization's
constitution and by-laws to avoid any future confusion
or dispute.

An executive committee can be particularly useful to an organization when its executive director is performing in an unsatisfactory fashion and a decision has to be made quickly and before the entire board is scheduled to meet. "It's important to keep the executive committee fully informed on the association's policy and the terms of any employment contract it may have signed with its executive director," says Siebenmann. "There should be clear notice provisions in the contract in the event you must dismiss an employee."

Sometimes personalities come into play and a conflict between the executive director and president of the organization prevent the organization from conducting business in a positive manner. I know of an organization where this issue caused the operations of the member-based association to come to a screaming halt because the executive director was terminated, the remaining staff quit, and the volunteer board could not even pretend to carry on as if nothing had happened. There was the threat of a lawsuit, pending police charges, and much more turbulence than any of the directors could ever have anticipated before they said yes to the call of volunteerism.

"The president of any organization should not act on behalf of the board — or as a CEO," says Siebenmann, "which is another reason to have an executive committee. It reduces the temptation and pressure on a president to act unilaterally and without consultation with other board members." This is great advice. Too often, we forget about the consultative process and its importance to the healthy and effective functioning of any board.

Siebenmann also offers a valuable tip when dealing with financial institutions: "It is important to be sure that the organization's financial institution understands that the authority lies with the board and not necessarily with the individual (staff) they may become accustomed to dealing with on a regular basis for daily affairs." It is therefore important to have co-signing authority designated to a board member even though staff alone may have the authority to sign cheques up to a specified amount.

Ideally, an executive committee of any board should:

- ✓ be comprised of at least three board members who reside in the same jurisdiction as the official office of the organization;
- ✓ fully understand the organization's contractual obligations;
- ✓ prevent the president or chair of an organization from acting without consultation or beyond the scope of his or her authority;
- ✓ follow up with other board members and staff to see that everyone is held accountable for designated responsibilities;
- ✓ have a set of keys to the organization's office and safe; and
- ✓ be able to keep the organization afloat in the event of unforeseen disaster.

"The best line of defence any board can take is to make themselves aware of any uninsurable risks," says Siebenmann. "Directors can be liable for unpaid salaries if an organization becomes insolvent. In my experience, that is an uninsurable risk that directors need to be aware of, as financial instability can increase temptations for wrongdoing to happen." That is extremely important advice that you (or designated representatives of the board) should review with your insurance adviser, as discussed in chapter 5.

"Most organizations work their way into financial crisis slowly and without intent," says John (Jay) H. Remer Jr., a North American consultant with extensive board experience. Remer has seen many boards through turbulent times and has some valuable insight to share. "The more inexperienced the board, the greater impact crisis (or perceived crisis) will have on them," he says. "I don't think it's a positive thing to plan for most disasters — other than a management dysfunction. But proactive thinking that focuses on policy versus crisis is definitely recommended." Remer goes on to explain that there are three steps a board should follow in dealing with unexpected problems:

1. **Recognize that there is a problem.**
2. **Identify the problem.** Is it *acute* — a flaw in the system that is non-recurring? Or is it *chronic* — a long-term, lasting, or repeating situation?
3. **Set up measures so that the mistake is not repeated.**

I can definitely relate to Remer's advice. In the situation I cited about my own experience with a board in crisis, had our organization more quickly identified that we had a potential problem with our former staff member, we could and should have put a plan in place to deal with a situation such as the unexpected departure of all staff. And as Siebenmann has recommended, had we had an executive committee in place, they could have acted quickly on behalf of the organization and prevented the board from being locked out of the office, without access to the information that was the heart and soul of the organization.

"There are going to be times when there are crises, and a policy has to be in place to help the board deal with them," says Remer. "The board must take measures to ensure that the organization is functional versus dysfunctional." This is not always easy. We are all human, and sometimes personalities and egos get in the way. The judgment of board members might be off-kilter because of their emotional involvement with the issue. That's where we have to step back and take stock of the situation. "You have to be able to separate facts from feelings," says Remer. "We have no control over facts, but we do have control over our response to the facts and the way we deal with them."

Once the board has clearly identified whether the organization is dealing with a singular (acute) or chronic (repeating) situation and all directors have checked their egos, emotions, and personal baggage at the door (along with their hats!) there is a much better chance of surviving whatever bumps might be encountered along the way.

My research on how organizations can best overt disaster led me to the Institute for Conservation Leadership and the Environmental Support Center who have jointly published a document intended to help non-profit boards be better equipped for difficult times. Their comprehensive report, entitled "Managing in Hard Times," can be viewed at *www.icl.org*. The advice you will find there is invaluable.

These organizations recommend that any organization should:

- ⇨ **take the initiative**. Plan for hard times during the good times. That way stress and emotions won't affect good judgment.
- ⇨ **ask staff to suggest a contingency plan.** What can be cut in the event that the budget has to be readjusted?
- ⇨ **identify core programs.** They are the heart of an organization. Then identify the core costs associated with those programs, knowing that these usually cannot be cut.
- ⇨ **seek strong board members.** They are likely to be determined and steadfast during tough times.
- ⇨ **openly identify authority.** Who has the authority to make tough decisions?
- ⇨ **focus on the vision.** Never lose sight of the organization's main focus when making tough decisions.

⇨ **keep the board fully informed.** Any problems should be addressed as they surface.

⇨ **identify problems and prioritize.** Determine which decisions the organization must make immediately and which can wait.

This is great advice that any organization or association should follow. Remember, it's all for one and one for all. With the right plan of action in place — one that includes preparedness, coupled with accountability and competency in directorship and leadership — board participation can be incredibly rewarding and integral to both our personal and institutional growth.

7   Are We Compatible?

We've talked about how boards work, about the different types of boards, planning and insurance for boards, and training and etiquette for directors. Now it's time to talk about you.

Why are *you* being recruited for this board? What do *you* have to offer? Do your personal goals and philosophy coincide with the goals of the organization? Are you and the other board members compatible? Is this a good fit for all players — you, the board, and the organization? These are the important questions we will look at in this chapter.

Why Me?

Board members are usually recruited for one of several reasons. Which one (or possibly two) applies to your situation? Be honest with yourself.

⇨ **Your profession:** Large boards will often have a couple of lawyers, one medical professional, one accountant, et cetera, on them and you are being recruited because you are one of those. That's pretty straightforward.

⇨ **Your constituency:** This may be in relation to where you live (a geographic representation) or it may be because you are a member of a certain group, political party, or organization that usually has (or is entitled to) a seat on this board.

⇨ **Your bank account:** If you have considerable wealth, power, or influence, you may be courted as a director for this reason — particularly by non-profit charitable organizations. No surprise here.

⇨ **Your age:** The board may be looking for fresh, young blood or ripe, well-seasoned blood. Do you fit one of these criteria and would your age-specific perspective provide an important addition to the board?

⇨ **Your sex or race:** There is often a deliberate decision to add more women to a board, to add more visible minorities to a board, et cetera. Do you think this is the primary reason you are being asked to take a position on the board?

⇨ **Your reputation:** You may have a noteworthy history, some special or unique ability, or a reputation for getting things done — being an excellent fundraiser, a conciliator, or a real people person, perhaps. Are your achievements and/or character the primary reason that you are being recruited for this board? This is always the most flattering reason for board recruitment and one that you should be proud of if the shoe fits.

⇨ **You're available:** This is the least flattering reason for being asked to say yes to a board position, but it happens more often than not. It's not always easy to get people to volunteer for board service and your name may have come up because you have a colleague, close friend, or neighbour on the board. Make sure you're providing more than just another "derrière in the chair."

It's important to learn why you are being recruited for a board, and to ask yourself a few questions: What specifically can I bring to this board of directors? Will my contributions be welcomed and considered valuable? Or will I be considered a necessary evil and someone whose opinion will not be truly valued and will meet with constant opposition?

It's really critical that you have this discussion with yourself and with the person who is recruiting you for the board, as it will help disclose the asker's expectations and motivations, and will also set the overall tone for the time you spend as a director. But just how long *is* that time going to be?

How Long Are You In For?

Now that you've (hopefully) figured out *why* you were asked to serve on this board, you need for find out for how long you will be expected to serve. Every board is different with respect to these expectations.

Generally speaking, you will be a more effective director if you do not limit your commitment to just one year. There is always a learning curve with respect to any board commitment, and sometimes it can be quite considerable. Leaving the board after only one year will not give you time to reach your full potential as a valued director. If you plan to serve what is expected as the norm on that particular board, you will be giving yourself time to fully understand the organization and its way of doing things. You will have more of an opportunity to become immersed in its culture.

If you join the board with the understanding that you have a lot to learn and will contribute much over time rather than the "guns a blazing" attitude that you are going to change everything in the blink of an eye, your time on the board will be much more pleasant — for everyone concerned.

Understanding why things are done is just as important as how they are done. If you take on the position of director with the intent that you are there to do the best job you can do, you will often find that your commitment to the organization will increase and become more meaningful for you. Increased commitment usually strengthens our willingness to hang in there and make a valuable difference to the organization. And that generally takes time — and more than a single year.

Board members who only stay for one year often don't have time to truly make their mark on the organization. And to me, that's a shame, as we all have something special and unique that we can bring to the table. But don't expect to do it overnight — unless you have specifically been recruited to bring a complete overhaul to the way the organization has been operating and have been given carte blanche to do so.

I have sat on a board where the unofficial expectation is for a director to serve four years. On another board, directors often ran for two successive three-year terms, making their board involvement a six-year commitment. That's a long time, but the work on that board was so varied and complex that it truly took the first three years just to get fully up to speed. It was during the second term that most directors truly shone and left their unique and memorable mark on the organization. In this type of long-term board commitment, you will generally be given an increasing amount of responsibility over time, and will come to know what you are good at and what you should avoid. I am terrible with numbers, so I've always steered away from committees or responsibilities requiring an aptitude for financial finesse.

Organizations such as Toastmasters International deliberately limit the terms of club presidents to one year unless there are extenuating circumstances and the need for the president to serve longer. But they permit you to serve in other executive roles for longer than one consecutive year.

So the key is to ask. Find out how long you are expected to serve on the board. Find out what the average length of service is for most directors. And ask if there is any protocol regarding the assignment of specific tasks and roles. Perhaps you will be able to have the role assignment you want if you ask the decision-maker for that privilege. Be proactive and enthusiastic in your role as a director. That way you will be a willing and knowledgeable participant versus someone who feels like they've been roped into something or confined against their will.

Finding a Good Fit

People who willingly take on significant board challenges inspire me. Tanya Gulliver is one of those people. After serving as president of the Professional Writers Association of Canada (PWAC) for one year, Gulliver volunteered to do it again and serve a second term! Not many people have that level of commitment, particularly after having already served a number of years on the board — she worked her way up to the position of president.

But volunteerism is in Gulliver's blood. Both her parents have been dedicated, life-long volunteers. And as a young girl, Gulliver was already active in student councils. She subsequently served on faculty council in university, became a school trustee, and has taken on other assorted positions — all while pursuing her university studies and, currently, her doctorate. So it's not that she had a lot of free time and is volunteering to fill a void. Why does she do it? Why does Gulliver spend so much of her time volunteering and sitting on boards?

"Each one has served a different purpose," says Gulliver. "I'm enjoying the PWAC board because I value the work the organization is doing. At the same time, I see my work on this board as sort of an internship — a way to learn more about the writing community." She also works on several other community boards that coincide with her personal beliefs and ideologies.

Has she ever found herself on a board that was not a good fit? "Yes, I've been on a dysfunctional board," she says. "The leadership and I could not agree on much, so I left the board." That is a well-stated course of action that I, too, recommend. Sometimes it *is* just better to walk away. You may believe strongly in the organization and be willing to give your time and help it achieve its goals, but sometimes the time just isn't right — because of the current leadership, or because of the climate concerning a specific issue.

If you find yourself on a board that is clearly not a good fit, resign — or at the very least, do not renew your term. It's better than banging your head against the wall. And if you really believe in the organization, wait a couple of years until the leader in question has served his/her term on the board and then get back on. The time may have ripened for you to be able to accomplish the goals you have for the organization.

What if *you* are the leader and are faced with friction on the board? How do you keep things moving and prevent the board from being stalled due to internal conflict? Gulliver has some insight on this as well. "People need to feel they are being heard," she says. "They are on a board to represent a constituency or to bring forth their beliefs and opinions. Too often, boards don't allow people to express their views. I try to make sure that they can do that, but don't allow for too much repetition either. I use my summarizing skills to summarize the discussion and have people focus only on what hasn't been covered."

I have heard that Gulliver has immense skills in ensuring that all directors are heard and respected. But that she also keeps the atmosphere light by instilling humour — like with the introduction of her monkey hat. "We were heading into a board meeting and I knew it had the potential to be challenging as a couple board members rarely saw eye to eye," says Gulliver. "As I was going through security at the airport, I saw the monkey hat and bought it, knowing that when I wore it, no one would be able to be angry because it was incredibly funny looking. It worked, because as tension at the meeting grew, I would stroke the monkey on my head and remind him to do his thing. Everyone laughed and got a bit more relaxed. I had some private discussions with both people as the day progressed and eventually things got better and both parties were in agreement on the important issues before us."

"Infusing an artistic board with some business vision can be a good thing, as it can create new ways of looking at things," says Nathalie Kleinschmit, who has served on a board with Gulliver. "Business plans are a necessary tool that can be fun and creative. They don't have to be a tragedy for artistic groups and other non-profits."

But it can be difficult to quickly change the attitudes and philosophy of an organization, and Kleinschmit's frustrations led her to resign from her role as a director after only one year. Her departure from the board did not alter her commitment to the organization or her willingness to provide input. "Sometimes it's best to provide input from the sidelines or as an independent consultant as opposed to actually sitting on the board," she says.

That is good and logical advice. You may find that your own way of approaching a goal is different from the majority of directors on the board. And you may feel like you're constantly swimming upstream when trying to further your principles or suggestions. If that is the case, it may be best to step aside and let the rest of the team do their thing. But that does not preclude you from providing input and drumming up support for your approach to an issue or strategy, and perhaps coming back to the board with a proposal once you have established that support — or perhaps even rejoining the board after the mindset of the institution has evolved and your original idea has made its way to the forefront.

Be patient, earnest, and be sincere. And if that approach doesn't work in establishing support, be gone from the board table — at least for the time being.

8   Let's Get Together

In the previous chapters you've learned a lot about the various types of boards and how you can prepare for your first board meeting. In this chapter, we will deal with the style, logistics, and frequency of board meetings.

Board Meetings

Before you say yes to sitting on a board of directors, you should find out the following information:

- ⇨ **How will business of the board be conducted?** Will it be primarily by in-person meetings, by email, or via web/video conferencing?
- ⇨ **Will you be expected to travel to in-person meetings?** If so, how often, and to where?
- ⇨ **Is video conferencing an option?** There may be times when you can't (or don't want to) travel great distances to in-person meetings.

⇨ **Will others on the board respect your own time constraints?** You may have other personal or business responsibilities.

Let's start with the last point. It's very important to determine whether the board you are considering is sensitive to the needs of individual board members. Some are, and will make every effort to schedule meetings that do not too severely disrupt the lives of the board members. Others are very regimented, don't like change, and are unwilling to alter dates and times of board meetings because, "It's always been done this way." Find out immediately what you will be dealing with — before you say yes to a situation that just won't work with your lifestyle or other commitments and obligations.

A requirement of board members to travel to in-person meetings can become a very important consideration. If you live in outlying areas of the country and most of the meetings are held in the centre of the country, you can imagine that you will be spending a day prior to and following the actual meetings in transit. Therefore two days of meetings becomes a four-day commitment. Will that sit well with your family, your work, or your other responsibilities?

You're Virtually There

Some people who do live a considerable distance away from meeting sites may prefer video conferencing as an option to on-site meetings. George Butters, a Fredericton, New Brunswick, technology expert and entrepreneur, volunteers his time and expertise for several national non-profit associations, including Child Find Canada and the Professional Writers Association of Canada. He is, no surprise, a strong supporter of video conferencing. "Having a half hour weekly meeting by video or audio conferencing can be much more productive that quarterly in-person meetings that last two days," says Butters. "Everyone knows that being away from home and the office for a number of days creates some form of stress and backlog for most of us. Using technology to hold more frequent meetings is less obtrusive and gets greater buy-in from a larger number of directors in my experience."

Although I am not opposed to an increased use of technology with respect to board governance, I have mixed feelings about it taking precedence over meetings that bring us together in the same room. There is something about sitting next to a person that will often give you greater insight into their viewpoints. Being face to face with someone does, in my opinion, create more of an opportunity for a true meeting of the minds to happen. And that, I believe, is the purpose of a board meeting: to reach consensus on a variety of issues so that business can be done and progress can be made.

For me, nothing can replace face-to-face contact. Perhaps that is because I am a real "people person." Being able to read someone's body language and having the opportunity to look into their eyes and read their sincerity is very important to me. It helps me gain a greater understanding of my fellow board members and helps me gain greater insight into their stance on any given issue. Perhaps that is a bit of a female thing. I think women are more in tune with body language. Butters agrees — to some extent. "I think there are people who are more visually intuitive than others and they may be somewhat resistant to video conferencing because of that," says Butters. "Perhaps females are more visually intuitive than males."

He agrees that video conferencing has its pros and cons. "There are always trade-offs, because anytime you adopt new technology, there is the law of unintended consequences that comes into play" he says. "You need to measure whether the benefits exceed the trade-offs."

Three reasons to incorporate a greater percentage of virtual meetings might include the following:

⇨ **Cost:** To keep expense of travel and meeting facilitation down.

⇨ **Convenience:** Some directors may find they are too busy to travel to in-person meetings, and it is also faster and easier to organize meetings when there are no flights, hotels, or meeting spaces to book.

⇨ **Conservation:** At a time when environmental responsibility is becoming more and more a pressing issue in today's society, this approach will lessen the environmental footprint of an organization by reducing fuel consumption.

Butters says that if an organization can live with the minimal shortfalls of virtual meetings, considerable benefits can be realized by the organization. "If you limit in-person board meetings to once a year — and I recommend it be the first meeting of the year to give directors the chance to actually meet one another — you can go online for the rest of the year."

Exceptions to that rule would be when the board is discussing highly contentious issues. "By not flying bodies around as much, non-profit associations can save themselves a great deal of money," says Butters, "particularly where the issues being dealt with are operational versus contentious ones which may be confrontational or divisive in nature."

For those more sensitive times, face-to-face deliberations work best. Think of effective contract negotiations. Effective bargaining or negotiating is almost always done in person because better results can be achieved when you are sitting across the table from the contrarians as opposed to across the country. It's much easier to say no or be obstinate in discussions when you are not directly feeling the breath — or the frustrations — of the other person.

However, technology has advanced to the point where people sometimes forget that they are not actually in the same room as the faces they see on the screen. "There are large, high-definition screens and special microphones that are located in rooms that are specially designed for virtual meetings," says Butters. "The technology is so real that I've actually seen people extend their hands as if to shake with others, and then realize they're not in the same room!"

These special facilities are often available for rent in mid to large size cities and provide a cost-effective option for large boards that are trying to reduce the cost of meetings while maintaining the positive attributes of face-to-face contact. They're quite a step up from simply having a web cam on a computer," says Butters. "And including an online chat feature for online meetings is a tremendously useful tool. You can send a private message to a participant for clarification on an issue while the meeting is ongoing without disrupting the flow of the meeting."

Butters' Tips on Embracing Technology

✓ Recruit at least two board members who are tech savvy or solicit the advice of at least two Information/ Technology (IT) independent experts to give their advice. (At least two are recommended because many tech experts are supporters of one platform based solely on personal preference rather than statistics or facts, so objectivity may be at risk.)

✓ Look for hybrid meeting models to provide a customized solution that meets the individual needs of your organization. (One size does not fit all.)

✓ Use technology to record meetings and distribute documents whenever possible. (It is cheaper, faster and more accurate.)

Butters and I agree that people who volunteer (or are recruited for) for board positions tend to be very busy. There is an increasing trend for directors to favour virtual meetings over in-person meetings, as virtual meetings are less disruptive to their already busy lives.

There are various technology options to consider. I've used Skype to put me "in" small meetings I could not get to due to inclement weather. Skype uses your computer's camera to put you in the room where the meeting is being held. As long as there is a laptop in the room, you can hear the voices of the participants, and if that laptop or computer also has a webcam, you can also see people or documents as needed as the meeting progresses. Skype is free (for the basic version) and very adequate for small groups to use. There are more sophisticated versions of Skype available for purchase. See *www.skype.com* for more information.

Other meeting software that is more sophisticated and frequently advertised on television is GoToMeeting. This company offers a free trial and three levels of service: online meetings for small groups of fifteen or fewer, webinars for up to a thousand participants, and customized corporate packages. For more information visit their website at *www1.gotomeeting.com*.

So it seems the days of in-person meetings are rapidly diminishing. Be prepared to embrace the new technology if you are a director; look at it as an opportunity to do things differently — for the good of the organization, and possibly for your own good as well. And if you are a leader or the chair of a board, be sure to remember the balance, and don't let technology take the "meet" out of your board meetings by making them too impersonal or robotic. Determining the right blend of technology and in-person meetings for your organization will be the recipe for success in the digital age.

Dinosaurs Won't Cut It

So what happens *between* meeting dates? How will business of the board be conducted? Faxes have pretty much gone the way of the dodo bird. It has been my experience that email works well for discussions on small boards of six or less members or for small sub-groups of a larger board. When you get into larger numbers of participants, however, electronic communication is simpler and more efficient with the use of a web board.

I have worked with a few different versions of web boards or web forums. These technological tools enable board and committee members to communicate effectively, and to keep discussion threads easily intact for future reference. They're a great way to store meeting minutes and resource material online for easy access by members at any time and at their convenience.

It is generally unnecessary for directors to purchase special software in order to access these web boards or forums. Most computers can access and handle the technological requirements. But if you do have to purchase software for whatever reason, the organization should pay all associated costs that enable you to function in accordance with the protocol of its board.

That doesn't mean that the organization should buy you a computer if you don't have one, or pay for a major upgrade if you are operating a dinosaur. But if you are operating a reasonably modern computer, that should be sufficient to serve as a director for most organizations. If your organization has higher standards than the norm, they should make that known to any prospective directors so that you don't take on a directorship, only to find out that you are expected to run a Macintosh 10.5 — or some even newer model.

There are certainly some small community boards that operate using only the telephone to communicate between board meetings and make little, if any, use of technology to handle board functions. But that is becoming less commonplace, and if you are one of the few directors who do not have ready access to email, you may find yourself out of the loop on daily or weekly discussions. That, in turn, may reduce your effectiveness as a director.

I have a friend who is an attorney and does plenty of work with boards. He refuses to use email. I can't quite understand how he can be effective at his work and be accessible to his clients when he is not making full use of modern technology. But that is his choice and I know he is well regarded for his services; to each his own.

I am not necessarily a strong supporter of the best and newest forms of technology. But I do like to take advantage of technological advancements that make my life easier and work for the good of my organization. Be open to options and to learning new technology, and you will find that staying on top of your board responsibilities can be a positive and enlightening experience for all concerned.

9 Show Me the Money

In the previous eight chapters, we have talked about board structure and key components of functionality. In this chapter, we're going to talk about board finances and approach a sensitive subject — one that has occasionally been perceived as the "elephant in the room." What's that, you ask? In my experience, the discussions surrounding board honoraria and directors' expenses incurred when travelling to (and attending) board meetings have often been contentious.

Why is that? Doesn't everyone believe in fairness? In most cases, yes, but fairness is an individual's perception of any given situation. We don't all perceive a situation in the same light, as we all come from different backgrounds and have a unique set of circumstances.

I believe that the difficulty in discussing honoraria is specifically related to the financial situation of each director. Some directors have prestigious jobs or hold positions that pay them handsomely, with generous benefits and considerable flexibility with respect to their time.

Other directors are self-employed (like me) or have modest means from which to live by. Out of necessity, we need to be reimbursed fully for our expenses and compensated for our time and effort by way of some kind of honoraria. I'm not suggesting that honoraria be considered "fee for service." That is not at all what I am advocating. It is our choice to volunteer and we shouldn't expect to bill organizations for our time when we are there in this capacity.

But I do think that giving our time, enthusiasm, and expertise are precious resources that every organization requires to exist and flourish, and that in turn, these organizations should offer fair honorariums to their directors — "fair" meaning as much as the organization can realistically afford.

If the director feels he or she does not need or want the money and would prefer not to accept the honoraria, he or she can donate the funds back to the organization. That solves the discomfort some may feel in accepting honorariums and does not create a situation in which some very qualified and eager individuals literally cannot *afford* to serve on the board.

What Is Fair?

What exactly is honoraria, and what is considered to be fair? The *Canadian Oxford Dictionary* defines honoraria as "a fee, especially a voluntary payment for professional services rendered without the normal fee."

The key word here is *normal.* The definition is implying that the person receiving the honoraria is doing so at a discounted rate that is less than the "normal fee" they would charge others for the service or their time. This premise applied to work I did for a group to which I belonged. I charged the association a token of what I would have charged a regular client to produce the same newsletter. I did this willingly, as a member, and was rewarded with a small honorarium to show value for my time.

Whether you are a director or volunteer member, you are doing the volunteer activity for the honour of serving on the board. And in turn, the board is honoured to have your participation and would like to reward you for it.

Every organization pays a different level of honoraria. There is not a norm, nor are there any formal guidelines for non-profit boards. Corporate boards are in a different league, and pay very significant honorariums (much more than I earn in an entire year). This book is about non-profit associations and organizations, though, and we will focus exclusively on them in this discussion.

You've gotten a sense about how I feel, but how do others perceive the payment of honoraria?

"Board participation should never be restricted to those who are affluent or who can afford — financially — to sit on the board," says Michael OReilly, a Thunder Bay communications consultant with extensive board experience. "Affording their time is certainly a consideration, but financial constraints should not be a factor in board participation."

OReilly has developed some strong opinions on this subject and I share them. "Boards should never seek martyrdom from directors," he says. "I remember being on a board in which the organizational culture made board members feel guilty if they asked for a raise in the honoraria. It should never cost you money to sit on a board, as you're already giving your time." Much of OReilly's board experience has been with arts and culture groups with smaller budgets, and volunteers who find themselves in the low to middle income range.

I share his sentiments and have personal experience that illustrates a scenario to which some of you may be able to relate. An organization that had been soliciting my participation as a board member had previously expected directors to pay much of their own expenses associated with attending meetings across the country. I literally could not afford to serve on that board because, as a self-employed person, I was already losing income resulting from time spent away from my home office.

The organization did not pay any honoraria to its directors — only a tiny per diem that was supposed to cover a portion of our expenses. It seemed ridiculous that I was expected to cover some of my own costs associated with attending those meetings — in addition to losing income by not being available for work during the three days I would be away from my desk for each quarterly meeting of the board.

Über-volunteer Gregg Hanson, who has extensive experience on both corporate and charitable boards, agrees — in part: "It's very important to pay all board members for any legitimate expenses," he says. "But with respect to honoraria, there's a real distinction between the corporate and not-for-profit world. It is not uncommon in the corporate world for board honorariums to be in the hundred-thousand-dollar range — in addition to meeting fees. But in the not-for-profit sector, I find that people are usually happy to provide their services for free, as most of them do it from the heart."

I have a big heart, too, but when I'm not sitting at my computer working, I have no income coming in. Therefore I, along with many other self-employed individuals, find that we have to restrict the amount of time we can volunteer — unless we receive some kind of an honorarium and have our expenses fairly reimbursed. For many potential directors, having a Christmas party or the occasional lunch just isn't enough of a "thank-you" to compensate for lost income.

Payment of Expenses and Honoraria

If you are fortunate enough to join a board that does offer you an honorarium and will reimburse you fully for expenses, consider yourself lucky. Most often, you will find that expenses for meals are subject to a per diem maximum. (Eighty dollars seems to be an average amount these days.) The per diem may be divided into three segments, with a certain amount applied to breakfast, lunch, and dinner. Or it may be a single flat amount that you will automatically receive for each day you were at, and travelling to and from meetings.

Some organizations are sticklers for receipts and will not pay any expenses until they are presented with the original copy. Others do not require an original copy — or any receipts at all. Be sure to find out how your organization works and what the expectations are to avoid disappointment, delays, and difficulties. "Keep all your receipts and submit them with your expense claims form so that there is no confusion and no delay in paying your claim," recommends Surendra Bungaroo, a former private sector auditor, now Associate Director, Finance and Administration for Access Copyright, based in Toronto.

In addition to meal expenses, many organizations will compensate directors who must drive considerable distances to and from meetings. Every organization will establish its own guidelines, but an average mileage rate is currently in the fifty-two cents per kilometre range. Some organizations also enable directors to claim for child care expenses and personal care costs associated with adult relatives for whom they are responsible. The key is to find out what expenses your organization will pay, what the limitations are, and when you will be reimbursed. Work within the system and respect deadlines that claims are to be filed by if you want to be reimbursed promptly.

Bungaroo says that organizations should develop easy to understand, user-friendly forms for directors to complete that allow for variations that may be atypical to the organization. He also says that it is important for organizations to succinctly outline the terms and conditions for payment of honoraria and expenses so that all is clearly understood by both the directors and the person or department paying the honoraria, and that the expectations are the same for both parties.

Honoraria will likely be paid in accordance with a predetermined plan. Sometimes it is paid annually, sometimes semi-annually, and occasionally, monthly. Expenses are generally paid immediately following meetings. It is reasonable to expect to receive reimbursement for expenses you have incurred within a month of filing your expense claim. I was fortunate to have been reimbursed for expenses within two weeks of filing my claim with an organization, but I have also had to wait six months to be reimbursed by another. Find out what the norm is for your organization so that you know what to expect.

Be aware that honorariums are taxable, and considered income by Revenue Canada. You may receive a T4 slip from the organization paying you an honorarium. You will have to claim this income as any other on your income tax. Honoraria is also subject to Canada Pension contributions, so once your honoraria has surpassed a certain threshold, CPP deductions will be taken from the amount you would normally receive. The total CPP deduction for the year will be shown on the T4 slip you receive so that it can be considered in your income tax calculations.

Financial Statements and Budgets

Another important financial consideration for directors to understand is how to read and interpret financial statements and to try and feel comfortable when discussing budgetary considerations.

"Money is a tool that any organization needs to know how to use," says Nathalie Kleinschmit, a consultant and trainer with extensive experience working with numerous boards and organizations. Kleinschmit says that organizations need to keep on top of financial matters in order to thrive, prosper, and remain healthy: "Too many times an organization's budget stays too much the same, even though the world around them may have changed considerably." So if your organization has changed considerably over the past year or two due to a spike in membership or a drastic change in funding or services provided, it is important for the board to sit down and carefully examine every budgetary line item and see what needs adjusting.

"If an organization grows too fast, cash flow can become a serious problem, as money going out for services may exceed money coming in from dues or other sources. This can create a cash crunch, and without careful planning, being a victim of your success can create organizational chaos," says Kleinschmit. It is therefore very important for organizations to ensure that each board member and key staff member has a basic understanding of how to read and interpret financial statements. This subject should be included in the board training and in the manual given to each new director, and also be a part of the training of key staff members such as the executive director of any non-profit organization.

A Few Budget Basics to Remember

⇨ The organization's annual budget is generally prepared once per year, but can be amended mid-stream if situations change drastically — for the good or the bad.

⇨ An income statement provides a time and place "snapshot" of the organization's financial position in relation to its budget.

⇨ Spend your time focusing on the net profit or loss, total revenues, and total expenses. Smaller line items may be of concern or interest, but don't let them hang you up; focus on the big picture.

⇨ Note which items are below or above their budgeted amounts; find out why the variations have occurred.

* Remember: always ask if you don't understand something. There are no stupid questions, and your query may spark an important discussion.

10   Playing Nice

You've learned the logistics of board involvement over the past nine chapters. In this chapter, I'd like to focus more on the interpersonal communications that are so much a part of serving on any board. If you're not a good team player and can't get along with other people, you cannot be an effective board member, as you will always be butting heads with your fellow board members and/or the staff of the organization you are serving.

Desirable Qualities of Board Members

In chapter 1, you were given a list of qualities that make an effective board member. They provide a good launch-point for further discussion on the type of personality and behaviour that will best serve any board.

Easier said than done? What if you are doing everything possible to get along with your fellow board members and/or the staff of the organization, but continually encounter problems because of a difficult personality belonging to someone sitting across the table from you?

This can indeed be a problem. It's certainly happened to me. I can think of one individual who was on a board with me who really liked to push my buttons. I'd say it was red, she'd say it was green — anything to disrupt the flow of the meeting and my train of thought. After all this time, I'm still not entirely sure whether she was intentionally being malicious, whether her intentions were good and it was just her nature to push past the point of reason, or whether her ego was the demon that persistently disrupted our meetings.

When you encounter a difficult personality, or "board bully," it's a good idea to try and determine the individual's personal agenda. Why are they on the board? What is motivating them? Do they have ulterior motives in becoming an insider to the operations of the organization?

A friend of mine (who prefers to remain anonymous) had as board experience that still troubles her when she talks about it. "I served with a couple of individuals on a school board who only took on board positions so that they could get the superintendent fired," she reflects. "Their mandate led to psychological, or more subtle, bullying. I can still hear one of them saying, 'Anyone in their right mind can see I'm right.' This kind of intimidation causes weaker board members to follow the bully and enables them to make selfish, self-serving decisions instead of [deciding] what is best for the organization."

My friend still shudders when she remembers how she felt on that board, and how the negative behaviour of others influenced her own (usually) good behaviour. "You've got to recognize when this is happening," she says, "and walk away before it causes permanent damage to your health, your family life, or your career. Backroom politicking is often dirty business and results in destructive, uncharacteristic behaviour. I know, as it was happening to me."

This advice comes from a very strong and intelligent individual who is generally not one to be walked over. So be aware that in your duties as a director, you may encounter individuals whose raison d'être is strictly egotistical and, very likely, detrimental to the board. If you get a sense this is happening, speak to someone you can trust before too much damage is done. There is strength in numbers, and by establishing consensus with like-minded individuals, you may be able to put the bully in his or her place. And if nothing can be done to stop the disruptive or destructive individual(s), walk away — resign from the board — before you become negatively affected.

As Jay Remer says in chapter 3 of this book, some people are just not meant for board work, but unfortunately that may not stop them from seeking it. These individuals refuse to check their egos at the door. It's always got to be about them. Their personal (but private) motto: "What's in it for me?" You usually can't change these people. They may be bright and have some terrific ideas or connections. That's fine. Allow them to be a member of the organization, encourage them to offer ideas, perhaps even ask them to help out on a committee, just don't ask or permit them to be on the board or in a leadership capacity if at all possible.

It will be one headache after another, as people with this type of controlling personality have difficulty if they are not completely in charge. The only good or right way is … you guessed it, their way! You will often see this personality type befriend weaker members of the board, as they feel it is a way to build their own power hold. Compare their mode of operation to the way Twitter or Facebook work. The more people you have following you, the more influence you can have.

In fact, I came across an interesting quote on leadership from a fellow I discovered on Twitter. Michael Hyatt is CEO of Thomas Nelson Publishers, Inc. and has posted some brilliant comments that I've read in the short time I've been following him *@michaelhyatt* and on his website at *michaelhyatt.com*. He writes, "Leadership is not about position, a title, or status. It's about influence." I absolutely agree. As a leader, you are bound to have influence, but in my opinion, the key is not whether or not you have influence, it's how you use your influence and for whose benefit.

If you have followed the line of thought I have been promoting in this book, you know where I'm coming from. Leave your hat and your ego at the door. It's one for all and all for one. It's about effective teamwork under great leadership that is purely for the good of the organization. A person with a big ego can't do that. They

Desirable Qualities of Board Members

- ✓ Be impartial.
- ✓ Be attentive.
- ✓ Be well-informed.
- ✓ Be innovative.
- ✓ Be fair.
- ✓ Be consultative.
- ✓ Be courteous.
- ✓ Be flexible.
- ✓ Be loyal to the organization.
- ✓ Be trustworthy.
- ✓ Be a good listener.
- ✓ Be there, by attending in-person and online meetings whenever possible.
- ✓ Be accountable for your assigned tasks.
- ✓ Be grateful for the good work of others.

can't put the greater good in front of their own needs. That person, therefore, does not make an effective or desirable board member. A board member with a big ego will provide the board's leader and staff with one difficulty after another.

It is very unusual for a controlling individual to change. An early warning of this type of personality is someone who bounces from organization to organization, usually with complaints about the organization they just left. That is a red light that this person is never happy and is likely to wreak havoc in your organization.

Dealing with Bullies and Difficult People

"When a fellow board member makes comments that are directed at you and you know they are trying to intimidate you, it's very difficult to carry on effectively in your role," says Joy Halloden (pseudonym), a Montreal-based consultant with extensive board experience who also prefers to remain anonymous.

It's interesting how both the women I interviewed for this chapter still involuntarily feel the effects of the board bullying they had been subjected to years before and fear for their safety or peace of mind should the bully be able to identify their comments.

The statement from Halloden above could just as easily apply to the staff of an organization. If key staff members are trying to drive the board, as opposed to carrying out the directions of the board, the organization is in serious trouble.

"The former executive director and a fellow director of a board I was on thought I could be bullied because I was too nice," reflects Halloden. "They thought I would be a pushover as chair of the board." The situation deteriorated to the point that the organization had a complete meltdown, lost both its staff members, and had to temporarily close its national office. "I felt like a deer caught in the headlights for a time, until I realized that I had to go into damage-control mode and draw on my inner strength to deal with the situation," she says. This involved getting legal advice, trying to keep members informed as much as possible without a functioning national office, and hiring a new executive director.

It is not natural behaviour for most of us to be confrontational. Most of us want and try to get along with our colleagues — some, like Halloden, to the point where being non-confrontational unknowingly and involuntarily caused damage to the organization she was dutifully serving. That's where the red light should be signalling from our inner sanctums. If it comes on, or you hear that little voice telling you to take action, listen to it!

Watch for warning signs that tell you something is wrong. The staff person Halloden was locking horns with was showing numerous signs that the situation was dysfunctional, but they went unchecked. The organization's key employee was working excessively long hours unsupervised and was running a part-time business out of the association's office.

But Halloden didn't heed the advice of those around her who expressed concern. And she didn't listen to her inner voice. "Even those of us who were raised in liberated families feel that we need to be polite," says Halloden. "And so when someone is being rude or bullying, we try to be nice and smooth things over. This doesn't work in controlling aggressive behaviour."

Halloden says the bullying incident was a turning point in her life, taught her to toughen up, and showed her how to become much more effective in her role as a leader. "The result of that situation was that we all grew through adversity," she says. "Lifelong friendships with other members of the board were made during the trauma that we had to deal with over the course of that year, and clearly the organization as a whole became stronger, as well."

Clearly, good can come out of bad situations, but unfortunately, bad situations can also lead to even worse situations — and occasionally, lawsuits. "Lawsuits are totally futile in that all they do is cost people and organizations money and often don't accomplish much, if anything," says Halloden, who knows only too well what difficulties can emerge when a lawsuit is pending against the organization you are serving.

How to Recognize a Potentially Litigious Personality

⇨   The person seems to know too much about the law (and may already have been involved in a lawsuit or two).

⇨   They want to give advice and affect change when it is not within his or her responsibility to make those changes.

⇨   They demonstrate the "bulldozer effect" and seemingly want to mow down everything and everyone in his/her path.

⇨   They have a negative personality and are always dissatisfied with things the way they are.

⇨   They enjoy manipulating the media.

My own experience has also had me come across situations in which, despite the fact that everyone's voice is supposed to have the same equal vote, concessions were made to smooth over one individual's difficult personality, and their voice was taken as being more important or influential than that of another person whose position was seen as of less perceived value to the organization.

This should never happen, and an organization that does let it happen is treading on dangerous ground — whether it is the danger of a potential lawsuit or word on the street that the organization is unfair or tainted.

Thankfully, the negative situations in board activities are far outweighed by the positive. Otherwise, you can be assured that I and countless others who have volunteered decades of our lives in support of non-profit associations and organizations would not willingly do so.

11 Keep Things Professional

For the most part, I've tried to keep the focus of this book very positive. But as we learned in chapter 10, there may be difficult people you will encounter in your board involvement. They may be bullies, or they may be individuals who show lack of good judgment and exhibit very inappropriate behaviour.

Dealing with Sexual Harassment

It's unfortunate, but it's out there, and you may find yourself the target of unwanted sexual advances or some other form of abuse from a fellow director or individual associated with the organization you are representing. Industry Canada tells us that allegations of sexual, physical, and/or emotional abuse by staff or volunteers of not-for-profit corporations are increasingly commonplace. Surprised?

Sexual harassment is defined by the Manitoba Government and General Employees Union as:

⇨ Unnecessary physical contact such as touching and patting;

⇨ Suggestive remarks and other verbal abuse or threats;

⇨ Leering at a person's body;

⇨ Demanding sexual favours;

⇨ Compromising invitations;

⇨ Unwelcome remarks, jokes, innuendoes or taunting;

⇨ Displaying of pornographic, suggestive, offensive, or other derogatory pictures;

⇨ Condescension or paternalism which undermines self-respect;

⇨ Physical assault;

⇨ Sexual solicitation or advance made by a person in a position to confer, grant, deny or influence a benefit or advancement to the person; or

⇨ Reprisal or threat of reprisal for rejection of a sexual solicitation or advance where reprisal is made or threatened by a person in a position to confer, grant, deny or influence a benefit or advancement to the person.

Does this unfortunate fact suggest that boards should address this issue in some way? Should the organization implement a screening process in which the personal history of a prospective director is checked prior to him/her being formally inducted as a director?

Should potential directors have to provide personal references before they are welcomed to the board? Would this requirement affect your decision to serve on a board? Be prepared for this scenario to occur — particularly if you are volunteering in an organization that serves the needs of children. For if there are an increasing number of situations arising in which sexual harassment or some type of abuse is occurring in non-profit associations, prudent organizations are likely already including some type of screening process or questionnaire in their board recruitment process.

In my opinion, that is good board practice. If you have nothing to hide, and your intentions are good and honourable, you should have no objection to a screening process being conducted by or for the organization you are volunteering to serve.

For a more in-depth look at the concept of board screening, I spoke with Holly Henderson, chief executive officer of Altruvest Charitable Services in Toronto, who told me that Altruvest is the only charitable organization in Canada dedicated to providing charities with the volunteer leaders and governance skills to help them become more efficient, effective, and accountable.

"Since our inception, over eight thousand individuals from over four thousand organizations have come through our governance programs and 66 percent of them are new to board service," says Henderson.

When it comes to board recruitment and screening, Henderson says the larger, more established charitable organizations are much better organized, with formal succession plans in place and nominating committees that act as screening mechanisms with respect to looking into the background, experience, and suitability of potential directors.

Henderson is very proud of the BoardMatch program administered by Altruvest that matches potential directors with the organization best suited to their interests, skills, and abilities. For more information, visit Altruvest's website at *www.altruvest.org/BoardMatch/Content/Home.aspx.*

Developing and Implementing a "Respectful Policy"

More than twenty years ago I was involved in the labour movement in Canada and attended many union meetings. I can remember several instances when foul language was used, sexual innuendos were heard, and there was some discomfort between men and women on the committee because of something inappropriate that had been said.

I'm certainly not implying that union groups have a higher instance of this type of occurrence than other groups, but my personal board experience has put me in this type of scenario more than once during my union activist days. And I'm no prude!

But what do you do when a fellow board member says or does something that makes you uncomfortable? How do you handle unwanted or unsolicited sexual advances? What do you do when a fellow board member uses crude or foul language around the board table? We'll try and address some of these questions in this chapter.

For some answers, and to see if anything has changed or improved over the past twenty years, I contacted Marlene Hubert, a former shop steward and now staff representative with the Manitoba Government and General Employees Union (MGEU). Back in the 1980's, Marlene and I had taken extensive union training and worked on many union committees together and were often the only two women in the room. She tells me that things have indeed changed — and mostly for the better.

"There are certainly a lot more women serving as shop stewards and involved in union activity than there were twenty years ago, so that has changed the dynamics in the room without question," says Hubert. "And we now read out a 'Respectful Policy' prior to educational events and conventions. This sets the stage for a more respectful atmosphere than in the days when you and I attended union events together."

The policy that Hubert is referring to is part of the "new" MGEU that no longer tolerates sexual comments or innuendoes — or sexual harassment of any kind. No wonder the female volunteer involvement has increased significantly. The union is now providing an environment in which its woman activists can feel safe and not have to ward off unwanted sexual advances or listen to crude language that certainly doesn't belong in any boardroom.

The "Respectful Policy" states: "The MGEU expects that interaction between union members will be based upon mutual respect, cooperation and understanding. As a union, we will not tolerate any form of harassment. Incidents of this nature will be dealt with in accordance with our attached harassment policy."

The backgrounder to this policy says: "Human rights and solidarity are fundamental principles of the trade union movement. Harassment strikes at both. Trade unions must work together to continue to protect the rights of all sisters and brothers. It is imperative we discard faulty stereotypes and learn to interact with mutual understanding and respect." The policy statement continues: "Harassment of any kind is a serious offense. The MGEU will neither tolerate nor condone behaviour that is likely to undermine the dignity or self-esteem of an individual or to create an intimidating or offensive environment."

Harassment is defined by the MGEU as any behaviour by any person that is directed at and is offensive to an individual. It encompasses — but is not limited to — harassment on the basis of race, sex, age, ethnicity, religion, sexual orientation, political belief, union activity, and physical or mental disabilities.

I commend the MGEU and other unions for taking a clear and strong position and formalizing a policy that leaves no room for the kind of naughty and sometimes disgusting behaviour and language that was commonplace during the organization's activities when I was on its board.

If you find yourself on a board that still allows off-colour or inappropriate language or behaviour from its directors, perhaps taking the MGEU's lead and policy language and applying it to your own organization would be a good idea. For permission and further information, contact the MGEU at *www.mgeu.mb.ca.*

If your organization doesn't yet have a policy in place to help you deal with a harassment situation but does seem willing to move in that direction, you may still have to deal with an occurrence on your own until a formal policy is in place. Talk to the offending individual. Let him or her know that their actions or language is inappropriate and unacceptable. If harassment continues, report the individual to the chair of the board by way of a formal written complaint, and threaten to resign if the situation is not corrected and resolved.

If the offending individual *is* the chair of the board, you may have to solicit the support of the remainder of the board in order to achieve results. And if that doesn't seem possible or likely, a call to the Human Rights Commission would be appropriate.

If you are thinking of joining a board that has an off-balance male to female ratio, or if you feel you might be the target of some form of harassment, finding out the board's policy on such matters — before you say yes — is a good idea. The world is changing in many good ways, but there remains a touch of inappropriateness and inequity out there, so watch for it.

"It's not to say that the 'Good Ole Boys' Club' is not still alive in the union movement — because it is," says Hubert. "It still rears its head in some ways, such as who gets to go to the golf tournament. It's always almost the men. It's sexual discrimination, but how can you prove it, and is it worth the hassle to try and do so?" In my opinion, probably not. But at least there's been significant progress made in the last twenty years regarding interpersonal communications between board members. And thank goodness for that.

Be the Best You Can Be

Over the first eleven chapters, we've taken a look at everything you need to know about boards — before you say yes to an invitation to join one. We've looked at the many positives of board involvement as well as a few of the negative issues you may encounter when serving on a board, and we have discussed how to best prepare for your new role as a director.

This final chapter will be a summary of some of the key points we have discussed which will help you be the best director you can be. We'll also help you identify your motivators — the reasons you want to serve as a director. And we'll give you some suggestions on how to find the right board, in the event that you have not yet been asked to serve as a director.

We'll provide you with tips on how you can plan for succession in choosing your replacement when your term has come to an end. And we'll wrap the package up with some personal reflections on how valuable board work can be — to the individual, to the organization, and to the community.

Let's start with the latter. I spoke to a well-seasoned former board member who provided me with words of wisdom she has gleaned from many years of volunteerism. "After a lifetime of working on boards, I decided they have saved a lot of marriages," says ninety-year-old Hope Spencer of beautiful Comox, British Columbia. Spencer has served on numerous healthcare boards in Canada and abroad, in addition to the boards of political agencies, garden clubs, and "too many organizations to recall."

"The act of serving on a board seems to give people permission to leave their spouses for a few hours, collecting bravos for their efforts. Sometimes, it is the breathing space the non-volunteer now has that takes some of the strain off the marriage. Particularly with respect to newly retired executives, whose wives may say, 'I married him for better or worse — but not for lunch!' How true that can be. We all need a time-out," says Spencer, my wise and worldly friend.

The key is to find balance. Too many times, volunteers delve into a project with so much enthusiasm that they exhaust themselves, leaving them with no energy for other areas of their lives. "It's terrific to support a good cause, but volunteers have to remember not to burn themselves out," says Spencer. "If you burn out, you're no good to anyone." It's true. We all have a limited amount of energy to devote to any given cause. Whether it is our relationships, our health, our sanity, our careers, or our bank accounts, something will suffer if you put too much of yourself and your energy into a single cause or organization.

If you are going to benefit emotionally, spiritually, intellectually, financially, or otherwise from your volunteer work without suffering from burnout, it is important to channel your energies to the right place. That means ensuring that the effort you are willing to put in will net the results you are looking for in order to feel fulfilled.

Another wise friend of mine is willing to share some techniques with us here that she has used to motivate employees in training sessions she conducts with her corporate clients. It's all about understanding what factors inspire us as individuals and what type of work or environment we need to be involved with in order to achieve personal, professional, or intellectual satisfaction.

The table on page 136, which she fondly refers to as "the P factors," is completely transferable with respect to volunteer work and board commitment. Thanks to Nathalie Kleinschmit of Global'Ease for sharing the following information. For more information, visit the organization's website at *www.global-ease.com*.

Identifying Your Motivators

Motivator	Underlying Feelings	What I'd Like to Be Given ...
Pay	I want to earn more money. I don't feel I'm earning enough money right now.	Cash.
Prestige	I would like more recognition. I would like to feel important. I'd like an opportunity to shine.	Corner office, car, and business card!
Power	I would like to have control over decisions affecting my work. I would like the freedom to do as I please.	Freedom ... and leave me alone!
Passion	I want to contribute to a project that is significant, that I can get excited about.	Involvement
Pleasure	I want to have some fun. I want to work with people I like being with. I want flexibility and low pressure.	A chance to smile
Potential	I want to use and develop my potential and share it with others.	A chance to grow

There is no doubt that the last three *p*'s, passion, pleasure, and potential, are the ones that most favourably transfer to volunteer involvement on a non-profit board. You are sure to gain great pleasure and develop your potential if you choose a board (or cause) about which you are passionate.

Power and prestige are certainly applicable, as well, but be sure that those attributes of board involvement are not your main reasons for taking on a volunteer commitment. Remember, it's all for one and one for all, so wanting to sit on a board to give yourself power or prestige are self-serving traits that may cause the board to be dysfunctional if not held in check.

And the final *p*, relating to pay, is something that would apply more to board involvement on a corporate board, for as we discovered in chapter 9, honoraria on some corporate boards can be quite generous and represent more income than many of us earn from our employment.

Pick Me!

What if you think you've got the right skills and motivation to make an excellent director, but no one has asked you?

It may be that you're not connected to the right people. Get out and join more organizations. Find out where you feel comfortable and where you don't. Not every organization will feel like the right place to expend your efforts.

Show your interest in serving the organization by volunteering to serve on a committee or help with a special event. If it's a good fit for you and you do a good job, someone will notice and perhaps ask you to chair a committee or event the next time around. And if that goes well, you may then be asked to consider joining the board. These things generally don't happen overnight.

You've got to become known as someone who is capable, passionate, and enthusiastic. Larger organizations may even have waiting lists for potential directors. If they do, ask to have your name put on the list of interested parties. Some organizations require that potential directors fill out an application. If you are serious about your interest, ask to have the application sent to you.

You will find a wealth of information about finding the right fit from an organization called Altruvest. They have a BoardMatch program that helps potential directors find the right organization to fit their talents and interests. Altruvest is not yet present in every major Canadian city, but their network is continually expanding and it is definitely worth making the connection with them if you are seeking a position on a board. To check out their website go to *www.altruvest. org/BoardMatch/Content/Home.aspx.*

Planning for Succession

So you've done a good job and your term on the board is almost up. Have you thought about who will take your place?

Sometimes we get so wrapped up in the job we are doing that we think we are the only one who can do the position justice. We think that "nobody does it better" than us.

Roy Yerex is a retired Manitoba lawyer who spent twenty-seven years volunteering on the same board, the St. James Historical Society, a non-profit organization that oversees the operations of Old Grants Mill in Winnipeg. Yerex was president of that board the entire time!

That may be a record of some sort, but I was primarily interested in speaking to Yerex because he now realizes he stayed on the board way too long, despite the fact that his intentions were good. He had thought that no one could fill his shoes, but in reflection, realizes he was wrong — his replacement is doing a stellar job.

"Being on a board means being able to pass the baton in a relay race," says Yerex when reflecting about when to step aside. "It isn't what people *don't* have; it's what they *do* have that counts. Enthusiasm can be enough to pull someone through a learning curve that otherwise might seem too much for them."

Yerex says that he has been very impressed with the woman who took his place as president on the board, as she did not have the formal experience he had thought was necessary to succeed in the position. "Energy and enthusiasm will get you further on a board than dog and determination will, any day."

He says that in most cases a dedicated volunteer will be able to make their mark and achieve their goals for the organization within the first few years.

"If you love the board, get off of it once you've made your mark. You'll likely have used your energy towards advancing a certain goal — and then it's time to move on." That is extremely important advice to remember as you move forward with your board responsibilities.

It's critical to plan well enough in advance to ensure that any upcoming vacancies do not catch you or the board by surprise. Start looking for the right replacement with plenty of time to spare, because like the search for a good or great employee, it's not always easy to find the perfect individual to join the board as a new director.

The Victorian Order of Nurses (VON), Canada's largest national not-for-profit charitable home and community care organization offers a forty-eight-page board manual on their website that suggests that recruitment should be a year-round activity for any board. It also recommends that organizations maintain an updated database of potential board candidates and their corresponding skills, and that former board members be used in an advisory capacity for the recruitment of new board members.

As an organization that thrives on volunteerism, the VON also encourages retiring board members to self-replace by suggesting someone to take the departing member's place well before their term has come to an end.

Even if it is not your individual responsibility to find a replacement, the nominating committee or chair of your board will likely appreciate any suggestions you may have for a possible replacement. Just remember, they are suggestions, and not a "given," as only the board or the organization as a whole (depending on the organization's constitution and bylaws) can ratify a new director.

Another interesting suggestion the VON has is for an organization to partner with another local organization (or several) with the goal of exchanging the names of retiring board members. What an innovative idea!

Visit *www.von.ca* for more on the VON's approach to volunteer recruitment as well as for a copy of their board member skills assessment form, new board member application, and sample exit interview questionnaire for retiring board members. The exit interview is an excellent tool that helps any organization better understand why individuals are willing to serve on its board. When an organization better understands why people are willing to serve, it can then focus on finding more similarly driven and skilled individuals.

Gregg Hanson has extensive board experience in both the corporate and non-profit sectors, including the prestigious positions of past chair of the Insurance Institute of Canada and the Winnipeg Foundation, and current chair of the United Way 2010 Campaign.

Hanson says, "The selection process is really key to director recruitment. Board selection in many organizations was more of an 'old boys club' in which current or retiring directors would refer friends, family, or colleagues. Today, it's quite normal for boards to do a gap analysis and see what skills we have, which we need, and which we're light on. We then cast a net and try and find exactly the right people who possess the skill set we're missing. Using a recruitment service is helpful in finding the right people and worth the effort."

That means not accepting the first name that is volunteered during the director recruitment process. "It's important for two or three current board members to interview two or three prospective directors. A proper selection process helps boards alleviate the likelihood of ending up with someone they don't really want," says Hanson.

Boards that have an effective evaluation process in place are also more likely to know what skills they are lacking and what they should focus on in the recruitment process. But sometimes things go wrong and mistakes are made. If that happens and it is soon clear that a new director is in the wrong place (i.e. doesn't fit in well with the board) the situation can be rectified with strong leadership.

"It soon becomes obvious if you have one or two individuals who do not fit well with the board," says Hanson. "If after sustained discussion you still can't reach consensus on an important issue within a reasonable time, the chair should call for a vote. It's then likely that the outliers will see they are outside the philosophy of the rest of the board and change their views — or perhaps even resign. Sometimes that's better for the organization as a whole than trying to fit a square peg into a round hole."

Occasionally, a board goes through a rough year, and would rather forget some of the difficulties they may have had. That's not always a good idea, as we should learn from our mistakes. And it certainly isn't fair to any new individuals coming onto the board.

Board veteran, "Joy Halloden" (a pseudonym) agrees. "It's important to ensure that your successor has been made fully aware of difficult personalities and any other problems you may have had to face over the course of your term," she says. Excellent tip from someone who earned her stripes the hard way and with little preparatory advice from her predecessor.

You've now got the tools and knowledge to venture forward and say yes to the prospect of being on a board of directors. I hope you have been inspired by the words of wisdom so willingly shared by the more than twenty individuals who have stepped up to the plate and enabled you to learn from their extensive experiences. That shows how the volunteer spirit transfers into every aspect of our lives and helps strengthen us as individuals and ultimately makes the world a better place.

I'd like to leave you with a checklist to ensure that you will be the best director you can be as you grow in the position. Good luck!

How to Be the Best Director You Can Be

✓   Take the training you are offered and become engaged in it.

✓   Do your research and fully understand the organization you will be serving.

✓   Respect board confidentiality.

✓   Be loyal to the goals of the organization you are serving.

✓   Accept criticism and learn from it.

✓   Recognize your strengths and your limitations.

✓   Participate in board discussions and be fully attentive.

✓   Be a good listener. Every director and member of the organization has the right to be heard.

✓   Have an open mind, be flexible, and learn from others.

✓   Be consultative. Do not act unilaterally — unless you are specifically authorized to do so.

✓   Take on responsibilities. Don't always wait to be asked.

✓   Be accountable for any responsibilities or tasks you have been designated or volunteered to do.

✓   Show gratitude and respect to fellow board members (or staff) who have done a good job on a project or task.

✓   Attend board functions that help raise the profile of the board or the organization. It's good public relations for all concerned.

✓   Try and get to know your fellow directors (and the association's key staff) on at least a semi-personal level. It will help you better understand their comments and positions.

✓   Be professional in your every action as a director.

✓   Be honest and helpful to your successor(s).

- ✓ Be careful not to burn yourself out. Enthusiasm and effort within reason is best.
- ✓ Know when to walk away. When the enthusiasm is gone, your ideas are stale, or you seem to be swimming upstream on every issue, it's probably time to resign, not renew your term, or find a replacement.
- ✓ Read this book from cover to cover, and recommend it to your fellow directors!

WEBSITES

Altruvest: Performance Improvement for Charities.
www.altruvest.org.

Encon.
www.encon.ca.

Global'Ease: Training and Consulting Services for
Your International Growth.
www.global-ease.com.

GoToMeeting: Online Meeting Made Easy.
www1.gotomeeting.com.

Harper Risk Inc.: General Insurance and Risk
Management Consulting and Administration.
www.harperrisk.com.

Imagine Canada.
www.imaginecanada.ca.

Industry Canada.
www.ic.gc.ca.

Institute for Conservation Leadership.
www.icl.org.

John H. Remer Jr., Consultant: Corporate Etiquette
and International Protocol.
www.etiquetteguy.com.

Manitoba Government and General Employees' Union.
www.mgeu.mb.ca.

Nonprofit Risk Management Center.
www.nonprofitrisk.org.

Official Robert's Rules of Order Web Site.
www.robertsrules.com.

PolicyGovernance.com.
www.policygovernance.com.

Santa Clara University.
www.scu.edu.

Skype.
www.skype.com.

Victorian Order of Nurses Canada.
www.von.ca.

Volunteer Canada.
volunteer.ca.

Of Related Interest

HOW LEADERS SPEAK
Essential Rules for Engaging
and Inspiring Others
by Jim Gray
978-1-55488-701-9
$19.99 £12.99

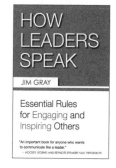

How Leaders Speak is a personal
handbook for planning and conveying
presentations that will engage and
inspire others, from overcoming nervousness to handling
difficult questions from listeners. In today's communication-
saturated age, the ability to address others effectively has
become the essential mark of a leader. Find the leader in you.

THE CANADIAN
SMALL BUSINESS
SURVIVAL GUIDE
How to Start and Operate Your Own
Successful Business
by Benj Gallander
978-1-55002-377-0
$26.99 £15.99

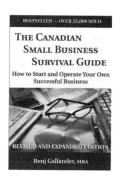

For anyone contemplating starting a small business with
potential sales of a few thousand up to the two-million-dollar
level, and for those who currently run their own businesses,
this is the most comprehensive, up-to-date guide available.

Available at your favourite bookseller.

DUNDURN PRESS
w w w . d u n d u r n . c o m